something BETTER

A Journey Through The Wilderness Into the Promised Land

melissa mattie

Printed in the United States of America

First Printing, 2018

ISBN: 978-0-692-17572-9

This book is a memoir. It reflects the author's present recollections of experiences over time. Some names, places and characteristics have been changed.

Edited by Rebecca Francis info@rebeccafrancis.org
Cover Design by Erin Herman

www.melissamattie.com

something
BETTER

PRAYER

11/8/2017

Papa,

I don't even know how to start this book. You tell us to be a witness to your power, and I know that's what direction you're taking me in, but to write an entire book about it? I don't feel like I can do that, but I know you can. Papa, I want this book to glorify you and to help ones like me. They need you Father. Papa, please help me, and let this book be completely Spirit-led. Give me the words You want them to hear. They need you. I need you. Thank you, Papa.

In Jesus' name,

Amen

Dear Melissa,

Use this book to write down your thoughts & poetry. You are blessed with the ability to write and who knows, someday you may be a famous Author! If not... You'll have poems or stories to pass on to your Children. I love you and am very proud of the wonderful Mother & Woman you have become!

All my Love,
Mom

Easter 2012

DEDICATION

I found this letter in an old journal of mine shortly after my Mother's death in 2015. I knew then if I ever wrote a book, this letter would be on the dedication page. You were right, Mama. I didn't find that letter until you were already gone, but it was a big factor in motivating me for this book. I made it.

I also dedicate this book to my husband and children. Rob, thank you for seeing me through all my spiritual battles while I wrote this book. I would be nowhere in life if it wasn't for your gentleness, kindness and unconditional love you have for me. To all my children, including my fur-baby, Cinna, I want to say Mama loves you all so deeply. I will always be there to help show you to your "something better."

I also want to dedicate this book to an author, Minister Henry Abraham. He wrote *How to Write a Book in 90 Day's God's Way*. Although I didn't follow your directions entirely, and I didn't finish this book in ninety days, your book helped me tremendously in the process of writing. In your book you wrote,

"One author who publishes a notable message may touch the life of one reader whose actions will impact the lives of thousands."[1]

I don't know for sure which person I am, but those words you wrote impacted me. Thank you for allowing God to use you in writing this book.

Most importantly, I owe this book to You, Papa. I wrote these words from the story you told. Thank you for trusting me with this story. Thank you for using me. Thank you for saving me. I will never forget how you showed me Something Better. I love you Father, more than I could ever express with words. Let's go save the world now, one reader at a time.

---

1 Abraham, Henry. *How to Write a Book in 90 Days God's Way: Empowering the Christian Writer to be Heard*. Xulon Press, 2008. Print.

DISCLAIMER

In this book, I have tried to recreate events and conversations from my memories. Human memory is flawed. It's almost impossible to recall a conversation word for word. I tried to be truthful in all my writing, and I apologize if it isn't exactly how you remember things going.

To maintain privacy and not embarrass the people related to some characters in this book, I changed some names and places.

Please understand, as I have learned to, that there is only one enemy behind the core of all evil.

Here is my story.

PREFACE

As I sit at my dinner table, there is a window right next to me looking out to the front of our house. I glance outside to look at the freshly fallen snow. It's December on the Eastern Shore, and the snow came in time. We are heading on a ski trip for Christmas this year. I've never been skiing before and I am smiling ear to ear, overjoyed in anticipation. We prayed for snow, and at first it looked like we might have to cancel because there wasn't a snow cloud in sight. I smile at how God answered in time, like always.

It's dinnertime, and my husband took over making food for the family while I practice my guitar for Friday night's worship. My ten-month-old daughter, Ember, is crawling on the floor looking for some mischief to get into. Briley, my oldest daughter, is sitting in the living room, captivated in silence by the television. It's her newfound favorite show. I don't know the name of this one, but I am sure it's some teen drama.

I pause and get out my notebook and pen to write this down. In a short while, we will build an addition to our home to make room for our growing family. My husband has it planned that there will be one extra room, and he has promised me I can make it into my library and office space. I excitedly told him of how I will use it. I would set up a desk and laptop and have space to write (or type, rather).

Blood rushes from my face as a thought comes to mind. It sends a fearful dread through my spine.

The thought that followed made me want to run for the hills: "I will have to go back into my past to write this."

How did I miss this important detail? I knew one day my life would be different, and I'd find my happy ending. And when I got here, the last thing I wanted to do was go back to the hell I came from.

I look up and glance through the window while my brows furrow in distress as a flashback comes to mind.

Not long ago I slept in my car in the middle of a winter like this one, with no gas money to run the heat to stay warm. It was so cold I could see my breath as I sighed and tried to cover up with extra clothes I got from my suitcase in the back seat.

I remember that feeling too well. No one cared. No one would even notice if I was dead. I was worse than hopeless; I was empty.

But then a reassuring voice quiets my racing thoughts and calms my fears.

"Yes, you will have to go back. But Melissa, that's where *they* are, and how can you help bring them where you are unless you go back and get them?"

I straighten up in my chair and get back to writing. I will brave this Journey, no matter what.

"You're right. I'm ready God. Let's go back and bring them home."

PROPHECIES

Feb. 12, 2013

1. You belong to me. I have named you and purchased you. Daughter, you are mine. You are not the property of any man. You are my possession.
2. I have called you. You will speak the oracles of God. My word will be on your lips, and you will declare it.
3. You will sing my praises. You will lead my people in worship. My songs will be upon your lips.
4. I have heard your voice. You were lost in a thick forest, but I heard you and am leading you out. Trust me, I have heard you.
5. Your daughters will be blessed by you. You will teach them to sing, dance and pray in my presence. My hand will be mightily upon them.
6. I will rise and defend you. The work I do in your life will amaze your accusers. They will ask, "Is this the same one we knew?" My work in you will be great.
7. You have been in a deep pit, but I by the strength of my hand am bringing you out. Trust me, Daughter. You are mine.

CONTENTS

one

IN THE BEGINNING

*"In the beginning, the earth was formless
and empty, darkness was over the surface
of the deep."*
Genesis 1:1

There are three times airplanes hold a significant part in my
life story. The first time was at the beginning of my life, the
second time marked one of the most traumatizing events I experienced, and the third...well, it hasn't happened yet. But I
have faith it will.

My mother proudly told me when I was a child that I had
first flown on airplanes when I was two weeks old. I always
thought it was neat knowing I had done something so young
when many people had never been on a plane before in their
entire lives. It made me feel special.

I wonder what my mother felt that night when she held me
in her arms while I lay fast asleep. She sat strapped in and holding me, waiting for the plane to take off. People were trying
desperately to find another available seat, so they didn't have
to sit next to the newborn. Hearing a baby cry was the last
thing they wanted to do on their plane ride all the way from
Florida to Michigan. Did she even notice, or were the anxious
thoughts in her head too distracting?

Was she scared, wondering to herself how she would do as a single parent? Was she strong and determined, trying to save me from the future she knew I would have staying with him? She had found child pornography in her husband's things and left him and her old life behind because, as I lay helplessly in her arms, she knew it wasn't about her anymore. Did she leave as soon as she saw it because she couldn't bear to think my father would... she felt sick to her stomach and shook the disgusting thought from her mind. She turned and looked out the window to hide the tears in her eyes from the other passengers.

With the plane now hundreds of feet in the air, everything seemed so small compared to the new life she held in her arms. That plane took us away that night in September 1987. She was thirty years old, and I had made her a mother. She wanted out of the partying lifestyle, and she wanted something different for me. So we landed into the state where her mother lived and into a new beginning for both of us.

My mother used to tell me stories about how her dad would take her to the bar every night when she was little and make her wait in the car until he came out. He would come stumbling back to the car, forgetting she was there and, by the grace of God, made the drive home without hurting them or others. She would quickly get inside trying not to get noticed and hid under her bed to avoid what was to come.

He was a mean, angry drunk, and a sailor at that, who definitely had the mouth to back it up. I only ever heard stories of him being drunk and angry and beating on my grandmother. My mother never told me anything about him hitting her or her other siblings, but I can only imagine how traumatizing that must have been for everyone.

I can understand the fear she must have had because before she had me, drinking and drugs were her life. When she met my father, she was a full-blown coke addict, and he was a coke dealer. They married and had me. Match made in Heaven, right? It wasn't until she found the child porn that she wanted to leave. When you become a parent, the last thing you want to do is repeat the same mistakes your parents made with you.

My father was furious at my mother, so he followed us. He rented out an old house not too far from where we lived. He tried to get custody of me, but it didn't work. The court granted him visitation every other weekend and every other holiday.

My parents were always so angry with each other, and I was always in the middle. It was a contest to see who the worse parent was. Mom would get angry about something my father did, and she would tell me bad things about him. I would worriedly brew over this until the next weekend when he would pick me up, and I immediately asked him if it was true. Instead of admitting it, he would try to outdo her and would say something like, "Well, your mother did drugs when she was pregnant with you!"

Feeling defeated, I slumped back in my seat and lowered my head down. Each time it happened, it left me with an empty feeling. And guilt. It was my fault my parents hated each other so much although I wasn't sure why. I don't remember ever feeling anything like "I wish I had something better," because this was all I knew. Sometimes I didn't even know if I belonged or if they loved me. I didn't even know who I was. I...existed.

So I became the "quiet child." At least that's what people said I was. I kept to myself and answered questions with one worded answers, not wanting to stir up any more conflicts or take anyone's side in the battles.

When both my parents stopped drinking and doing drugs, they focused on other relationships to fill their voids. This is where I learned to fill my voids too. I so desperately wanted to find love and acceptance, so from the time I knew what a boyfriend was, I have never been without one. With each boyfriend, I changed myself into what I thought he wanted me to be like. If he cussed, I was right there with them. If he wanted a lady, I acted like I had never cussed in my life. Whatever type of music he listened to was suddenly my favorite type. This became an ongoing cycle in my life, defining myself through my boyfriends.

In elementary school we worked on the infamous "What I Want To Be When I Grow Up" project. We sat at the computers to start our research, and as everyone excitedly typed away into their web browsers, I sat there completely stumped. I heard kids around me proudly proclaim, "I am going to be an astronaut and fly my spaceship to the moon!" or "I am going to be a doctor, like my dad!"

And another, "Well I am going to be a police officer and keep the bad guys off the streets!"

I sat there trying so hard to figure it out, and absolutely nothing that came to mind sparked my interest.

My teacher noticed the concerned look on my face and came over to intervene.

"Do you need some help sweetie?" she said with a helpful smile on her face.

"I don't know what I want to be when I grow up." I slumped back in my seat.

She smiled and reassuringly said, "Ok, well what are things you enjoy doing?" I shrugged my shoulders and said the five words I have said my whole life from that point forward.

"I want to help someone."

She got a proud look on her face and said,

"I know what you should be. You should be a nurse."

That was it! I could be a nurse. In fact, I would LOVE to be a nurse! They care about people and have a heart for helping, and that's what I wanted to do, to help the world! I turned around to my computer and worked.

As the years passed, my mother and father's anger towards each other took effect on me, which caught their attention. I became the "problem child." There was always something wrong with me, according to them. I was in and out of therapy and psychiatrists. I would blow up in anger and yell, then lock myself in my room and cry. They looked at me with displeased judgment, like they couldn't think of where I got this from.

I was still actively trying to fill my voids, and at thirteen, I had my first taste of alcohol. I didn't know what it was or what it tasted like, but I wanted it, and I wanted a lot. I learned I had an addictive personality. I got addicted to anything that made me feel better.

By this time my mother had married a third time to a military man who controlled her life. He was stationed down

South, so once again we packed up and moved. He wanted no part of anyone who would bring any disorder to their lives. So my mother convinced my father to take me, and in exchange, she would write off all the unpaid child support he owed. He agreed. They sent me to live with my father, who by this time lived in Maryland and had remarried.

I got to feel what people mean when they say, "red-headed stepchild." I came into the lives of a new family: my father with his new wife and her two children, with one more child on the way who was my dad's. I had a "boot camp" chore list already waiting for me, which Dad liked to call, "Raising you the right way and fixing your mother's mistakes."

I was fifteen and spent the time I wasn't in school doing dishes every night after cooking all the meals for the family. I had to cut all the many acres of grass my dad had with a push mower, with no motor, at least once a week. I wasn't allowed to go on family outings, not even to McDonald's. Using things like the phone or watching TV were out of the question for me. If I didn't do these things, my dad punished me. This was when my dad became physically abusive towards me.

One night he said something I'll never forget. I went outside to give him a hug goodnight and then walked back into the house, about to go to bed. He came storming in behind me with an annoyed and angry look on his face.

"I know what you're trying to do. You're trying to make me choose you over her, and I choose her any day!"

My mouth dropped in shock and nervousness, "I-I-I was giving you a hug goodnight, I-I-I don't understand!"

His demeanor changed, "Oh. Well, don't interrupt me when I'm outside talking to my wife. Get to bed."

I quickly turned around and ran upstairs to my room. I laid on my bed staring at the ceiling trying to process what happened. Sometimes those words still ring in my ears all these years later. Mental abuse is the worst kind. Bruises come and go, but words will haunt you forever. So I became a choice that no one wanted to choose.

One night as I finished up the dishes from that night's meal, my father was in the next room on the computer. He turned to look at me. His face showed his annoyance with something, so I held my breath to brace myself for what was next.

"You're too lazy. Why don't you try out for a sport or something?"

Wanting to gain his approval, I knew the cheerleading squad at school was having tryouts, so I thought it was worth a try. Unexpectedly, I made the team, and I couldn't wait to come home and tell my dad the good news! I rushed off the school bus and into our side door where he was standing next to our birds' cage.

"Dad! I made the cheerleading team!"

He looked at me in disgust,

"Great, now all my neighbors will know what a slut my daughter is."

I always looked in the stands at the football field when we had a game. I thought for sure he would come to one to see me cheer even if he didn't approve of the sport I had chosen, but he never showed. Because he didn't give me any money for things like school clothes, supplies, or my cheerleading uniform, I bought them with money I begged my mother for or earned working during the summer.

Many days I went to school wearing long-sleeve shirts and jeans in eighty-five-degree weather to hide the bruises from the night before. I never told anyone. I became good at putting a smile on my face even when I was dying inside. When I tried to tell my mother about it, she didn't believe me, so who else would believe me, anyway? I learned to suck it up and stop being a baby about it.

I don't remember why my father was so angry with me to make him want to drag me up the stairs by my hair. Hysterically crying and screaming, I struggled to get out of his grip. When we made it to my room and he put me down, I put my hands on my head to soothe the pain. He waited until I got to my feet, and he shoved me back down. I hit my head on the bunk bed behind me, and it was hard enough to knock me out. I shook awake in confusion to him standing above me with his arms crossed, kicking me, telling me,

"Stop faking it."

One night I grew brave enough to run out of our side door away from him. I ran to my neighbor's house. Mark and I attended school together, and we were in the same grade. With all the yelling next door, he knew what was going on. He opened the door with a concerned look on his face.

"Are you all right?"

"I'm fine." Typical answer of mine.

I saw the flashing lights out his window.

"Crap, my dad called the police on me. I better get back."

I walked back into the house. The officer was standing near the door with both arms on his hips while my father told him how psychotic I was and that I ran away.

The officer turned to look at me and asked me if this was true. I put my head down in silence. He asked my father to give him a tour of the house, and after a few more words back and forth, he announced that he was leaving and that he was taking me.

I cried but didn't dare argue and followed him out to his car. Because there wasn't a struggle, he let me sit in the front passenger seat with him instead of the back. He buckled me up and came over to his side, and as we backed out to leave, he turned toward me gently.

"You don't have to say anything. But I want you to know I took one look at your father, one look at the horrible conditions of that house, and then one look at you, and I knew what was going on. Do you have anywhere you can go tonight, any family or friends?"

After I finished telling him about someone's house I could go to, I turned to look out the window to process what he had said. We spent the rest of the drive in silence, but my thoughts were loud and anxious while I replayed what he said. I never said a word to him about my father or what was going on, but I'll never forget that man for believing in me even though I didn't say a word.

The next day I got onto a plane to fly back to my mother's house. She agreed to let me come back and bought me the plane ticket. Not much had changed, and they kicked me out two weeks later, sending me on a plane back to my dad.

I saw this coming. I didn't even finish unpacking my things because somehow I knew I would need them packed again.

I landed at the airport back in Maryland and waited at baggage claim with my one suitcase. I was numb and worn out. I didn't notice that I sat there for a while waiting. Two hours turned into five hours, which turned into eight. I wish I could say I was worried, but this wasn't a surprise. I told security what happened.

"No one is here to pick me up."

A young adult male turned his head from side to side, not sure if I was speaking to him or if there was someone else there with him. He saw it was only him.

"What do you mean no one's here to pick you up? Are they late?"

I told him the whole story of how I got taken away from the police to move back to my mother's, to move back here to my dad's. I told him he didn't come to pick me up from the airport probably because he didn't want to. That got his attention, and he realized it was a serious situation. He asked me to please take a seat and made a phone call.

I fell asleep in the chair waiting and woke up to a gentle-looking woman with glasses on the brim of her nose and curly brown hair smiling down at me.

"Melissa?" she said as she slid her glasses back up her nose.

I shifted in my seat and blinked my tired eyes awake. "Yes. Who are you?"

She brought her hand out to shake mine and introduce herself.

"My name is Patty. I work with Department of Social Services, and I am here to help you. So can you tell me a little more about what happened to you? It's a long drive once we leave here, but I have a family that can't wait to meet you and..."

My attention drifted off into the realization of what was happening. That day was the day they put me into foster care. I had turned fifteen. That was the day I realized that I was right. Without a doubt, no one wanted me. I was the choice no one wanted to choose.

two

SOLD INTO SLAVERY

Jesus Replied, "You do not realize what I am doing, but later you will understand."
John 13:7

It didn't take long for me to jump from home to home and school to school. I was a troubled teenager, and no one wanted one of those. I didn't care about anything anymore. I was going through the motions of things. I skipped school, tried out drugs, and let my foster brothers do whatever they wanted to me. I felt dead and hopeless inside.

My mother and father apparently didn't fight to get me back. I talked to my mother about it once; she said she thought this was the right thing for me, that they could "help" me. After being kicked out of my last foster home, my social worker went to court, and the judge proclaimed that I was "unfit for society." Even "society" didn't think I belonged.

They shipped me off to a residential treatment center, called Chesapeake Youth Center, before my sixteenth birthday. It was much like a psych ward, but you lived there and went to school there. There were twenty females, and we were separate from the twenty males who lived in the other wing. A card, which only the counselors had, locked and protected all the doors. A nurse sat in the nursing station waiting to give us our next dose of the bi-polar medication the doctor had us on. We were on a leveling system: Gold Star Level was for the ones that were "faking to make it," and the Suspended Level was for those who broke the rules and acted out, having to eventually end up getting a Thorazine needle (horse tranquilizer) shot by the nurse in their butt.

I quickly made it up the levels to Gold Star a couple months after being there. On this level, you get to go on outings with your counselor and do fun things. On our first outing, we went to a skating rink where I had worked in the past, and I knew the people and area well. I knew I would make a run for it. I wanted out of this place, and I didn't care what happened to me. When the counselor wasn't paying attention, I took off my skates and ran. I didn't look back until I knew I was safely out of vision.

A family of one of my old coworkers took me in. They didn't seem to mind that I was a runaway. They even got me a carton of cigarettes. I don't remember if I ate anything or even showered. I remember staying high the entire time.

We were in the car on our way to Annapolis to get the harder drugs when we stopped at a store to get stuff for the car ride. I stupidly thought it would be okay for me to go inside the store, thinking no one would see me, but I was wrong. A counselor from the treatment center was there down an aisle shopping, saw me and called the police. Only four days later, the police found me and took me back. Honestly, it was a blessing in disguise because as reckless as I was, as soon as I got my hands on more drugs, I would have tried all of it, not caring if it killed me.

They took me back to the treatment center and immediately put me on AWOL Risk. I got moved to the "Quiet Room," a room with no windows or furniture, cement walls and a door bolted from the outside. I had a mat on the floor on which I slept, and they took my shoes and my clothes. They gave me a yellow jumpsuit to easily spot me if I tried to run again. I spent eleven months on AWOL Risk. I couldn't leave, not even to go to the cafeteria. I didn't see or smell the fresh air from the outside world for eleven long months.

A POEM I WROTE IN CHESAPEAKE YOUTH CENTER

She's not real, they know they're not wrong,
She's from a different world, there's nowhere
    she belongs.
Her mom and dad are gone, and no one ever
    sees her cry
They wonder what day she will decide to die.
They never gave her a chance when she walked
    through the door
Not one little glance
She sits in the back of the room by herself
You won't ever see her raise her hand and ask
    for help.
You can't see me, hear me or feel me. I have
    no fear
Because I am not real.

After one month short of a year, I will never forget the day they let me off AWOL Risk. A nurse, Ms. Darlene, had grown to like me. She was a sweet, short, older lady who wore a cross around her neck. She had short curly hair and glasses, and if I would have known Jesus, whom she displayed on her necklace, then I would have known for sure she was one of His children because there was something about her that drew me in. I can't explain it other than I felt safe. She came up to the Quiet Room, that was close to the nursing station, with tears in her eyes and a smile. I saw her facial expressions and immediately cried because I knew what she would say.

"No! Am I off? It can't be! Oh my God, please, tell me!"

She nodded, and it seemed like it brought her as much joy as it did me. She tried to hide her tears, but they flowed more.

"Come on Melissa, let's go outside," she said as she tried to sniff back the tears.

We walked in the courtyard. The courtyard was an outside area in the middle of the building, enclosed on all sides, but I have never felt freer in my life than at that moment. I sat in the grass for what seemed like hours soaking up the sunshine on my skin. Rushes of all kinds of emotions flew inside me, but most of all, relief. I don't remember what month it was, but it was warm out, so it must have been spring or summer. It was warm out last year when I ran. Did I really spend an entire year in that room?

I am thankful I had Ms. Darlene there. She must have been my guardian angel. But having her shielded none of us from the hardships we endured. Shutdowns happened all the time from someone acting out. Down the hallways I heard endless crying throughout the night. One roommate I had tried to cast a spell on me. She drew herself in a Pentagram, spoke gibberish, and looked with evil eyes towards me with her arms outstretched. One time I was walking down the hallway to go into my room when four girls coming from both sides came after me and jumped me. What for, I still don't know. I heard a story about one of my old roommates getting raped by a counselor there. I'm not sure if it was true, but nothing surprised me anymore. We were guinea pigs there for the doctors to test out all sorts of medicine. Many times someone tried killing themselves, including me. I would save up Thorazine pills to overs-dose with or try to make a tool to cut my arms with. It was complete turmoil. I wonder if Hell is like that. The Bible says there will be weeping and gnashing of teeth in Hell. Well, when I look back at it, that sure seems like it was close to what I felt. No matter what happened though, something told me to keep holding on, that there has got to be something better than this.

They discharged me a month before my eighteenth birthday. Turns out the facility got shut down not long after I left. Someone must have found out about the cruelty with which they treated us. I went to live in a group home not too far away for the rest of my time as a minor. The night I turned eighteen, I signed myself out of the state's custody at exactly 12:01 AM. I walked out of the group home doors with my one suitcase and a little of the state's money left over. I didn't care what was next; I just wanted this chapter in my life to be over.

I moved back to Michigan where I had family on my mom's side. It took getting used to being on the outside again. It was strange and intimidating; I still felt fifteen, like the years froze in between. High school was too difficult for me socially, so I finished up my schooling in an alternative school. Having a mental illness and taking bi-polar medicine made me feel different and like something was wrong with me. There was nowhere I fit in. I still had the lowest of lows and depression still had its hold on me.

In this World 3/14/06

Depression overrides me like a claustrophobic girl.
Never being happy, but I know what I have to do in this World.
I don't want to be high or to smoke away my sorrows.
Even if it gets me through this day, what would I do tomorrow?
I have a lot of dreams, and I always keep the faith,
But how can I accomplish anything if I can't keep up the pace?
I thought being alone was my only biggest fear,
But now I know I'm not happy with myself when I look into the mirror.
All I wanted was to be happy and to prove others wrong.
But to keep on going would be way too long.
But like I said I'll never give up hope or to mouth a silent prayer
Because if everything comes true, I'll keep on wishing if I can get it later.
I know to be patient and to keep my head up high
Even if my whole life has been one big sorry lie.
I don't want anyone's sympathy or to look down on me.

I'm a big girl now, I don't need anyone so it's
best if you leave.
They say I'm contagious and I don't want you
to get sick.
Because to hurt others is not worth it so I'll
dwell in my own loneliness.
Why did I drink the alcohol and mix it with
the pills
Now my systems crazy and I'm heading for
the hills.
Depression overrides me like a claustrophobic
girl
Never being happy, but I know what I have to
do in this World.

Still trying to fill voids in my life, I got back in touch with a guy I dated in high school back in Maryland. We immediately clicked back together, so I packed up the car my grandmother helped me get and moved back to Maryland. I wanted a family so badly. I often thought to myself that if only I had a child and family, then someone would love me who would never leave me. I got pregnant not even a month after us getting back together and had a beautiful baby girl. I hoped for a girl, maybe so I could have something with her that my mother and I never had. She became my world, and things weren't about me anymore.

But her father and I were moving in different directions, so I left. I went on to a second serious relationship and another baby girl, which didn't work out either.

Nothing I tried worked. I moved from place to place thinking a new house would give me a fresh start, but never once did I feel like I had found a home. Since turning eighteen, I had moved eight times. It felt like I could never unpack that suitcase. I couldn't keep a job. I became a mess, drinking heavily when I put the girls to bed and sometimes going for days without a shower. I realize now that I chose men like my father, controlling and full of anger. I was nothing, a nobody. I tried to be a good mother, but I wasn't any good for my girls. My life had no meaning, no reason.

"NUMB" 4/11/2012

Numb, an emotionless emotion

Every day you feel like you're going through
the motions

Crying seems appropriate, but your bodies
dehydrated and there's nothing left.

Do you fake a smile or let out a laugh?

When all else fails to you act mad?

How can you when you remember how it used
to be and that happiness you once had?

When you're feeling numb happiness is like a
needle in a haystack you'll never find

You can try, but numb means there's no hope
left in your mind.

How do people get to numb and get to this
point of black and white?

More importantly, how can you see color
again; when everything was right?

But was it ever in the first place?

You see numb makes you see differently in a
constant mind race.

You lie down and wonder if it will ever go
away, alone in the dark.

And try to ease your breathing, but the pain
is too much from the pounding of your
heart.

Maybe that's what numb is a pain so deep it
went into shock,

Life support can only help so long so now it's
a race against the clock.

Either way, I guess it's something I'll never know

But like an endless game of Monopoly, I never
pass go ,straight to this jail straight to
numb.

This emotionless emotion, going through the
motions.

One I'll never be able to outrun.

UNTITLED 4/25/2012

I want me to finally matter.
I'm worth so much more and I've fallen and
    gotten back up countless times on life's
    long ladder.
I've lost myself, maybe somewhere along the
    way
It's like I keep picking up where I left off, the
    page is bookmarked
Like I'm molding and reinventing discovering
    new things in my heart.
More than what you think, more than what
    you know.
There's a side of me I keep locked up, Some-
    one I've never shown.
Insanity; doing the same things expecting dif-
    ferent results
I want a life worth having knowing it's a life of
    no regret; a life of no fault
I think it's time for the broken record to stop
    and the reinvented to become resurrected.
Someone once told me I was born to be a
    mother
And until the day I die those words will stick
    like no other.
To be wanted to have a purpose and to be
    needed
It's all I ask for in life it is all I've ever pleaded
To know I was born to be someone and to say,
    "I was her."
That's all it takes and finally...I matter.

One night, in November 2012, while my youngest daughter's
father was working an overnight shift, I started heavily drinking after I put the girls to bed. I was smoking a cigarette outside on the porch, which was on the left side of our house. I
stared at the ground. I'm sure if I had seen myself, I would

have thought no one was home. Blank, I had not one thought to wake me up inside. I felt like I couldn't go on much longer. I got on my feet, stumbling to get back inside and go to sleep. If I could sleep, then I would forget about being awake. That idea seemed much better.

Before I went back inside, my legs grew weak and I fell to my knees in defeat right there under the night sky. I had heard of God, but that was all. I had no spiritual guidance when I was growing up and no one in my family were churchgoers. I didn't know if God was real or if He even existed, but I felt like I had nothing to lose. I picked my head up and looked to the night sky. Out loud, in complete anguish, I cried out to God hoping He was real:

"God, I don't know if you can hear me. I don't know if you're real. But if you are and you can hear me, then please, I need you to help me. I can't keep living this way. I'm so sick and tired of being sick and tired. I am sorry for the way I have lived my life. Please, if there is any way you can, please... help me."

As soon as I finished, a thought immediately came to mind, "Tonight is Saturday. Tomorrow is Sunday. Go to church."

I didn't know what to think, so I shook it off. I got up and walked downstairs and went to bed. The next morning when I woke up, I wasn't going to go to Church, but I was talking to my mother on the phone that morning and she convinced me to go. Maybe I needed time alone without the kids. So I went alone and left the girls with Mark. I remember talking out loud the whole ride, pleading with God:

"Please show up, please show up."

Let me tell you, He sure showed up! On that day, November 4th, 2012 my life was never the same! He showed up in a way I could no longer deny His existence. I was in complete awe. I spent the rest of church service on the floor trying to comprehend what happened and why I was there. I have seen people "fall out in the Holy Spirit" before, but I didn't believe it. It always seemed like witchcraft. But here I was, on the floor with no idea how it happened. When the pastor laid his hands on my head, I put my hands up like I was surrendering.

I didn't know why I did it. Immediately a rush came through me, like tidal waves throughout my whole body, starting at my feet all the way out of my head. It was like something was being pulled out of me. Was I delivered from demons that tormented me with depression and bipolar disorder that day? I don't know for sure, but I can tell you since that day I never felt the angry outbursts or lows like I once felt before. They were ....gone. Over. Done.

I came back to tell my fiancé, Mark, but he and his sister made fun of me in disbelief. His sister Alyssa laughed obnoxiously. "Ha, Ha! Crawl to the altar?" She turned her head from side to side. "Pfft, you probably don't even know one verse in the Bible!"

They both leaned against the counter in the kitchen with their arms crossed laughing at me. It hurt, but it didn't matter even if she was right about me not knowing a single verse in the Bible. I knew what happened, and I would forever treasure that moment in my heart for as long as I lived.

I grew on fire for God. It's like when you first fall in love with someone, you can't stop thinking about them. You talk about them all the time, and you want to know everything there is to know. God set me free, and I wanted to know Him and follow Him no matter the cost. He was real, and somehow He chose a girl like me—when no else did.

I ended up leaving Mark shortly after. As much as I would love to tell you the hard struggles ended here, little did I know, this was only a beginning.

three
FOLLOW ME

Then Jesus said to his disciples, "Whoever wants to be my disciple must deny themselves and take up their cross and follow me."
Matthew 16:24

I remember watching the movie *Labyrinth* with David Bowie in it when I was younger. It must have been one of my favorite movies because I remember watching it constantly. A girl, named Sarah, made a wish for the Goblin King to take her brother away. Much to Sarah's surprise, her wish came true, and now the only way to save her brother from the Goblin King was to go in the maze and find him herself. The Goblin King didn't make things easy for her. There were plenty of traps and distractions and creatures that lived in the maze that tried to entice her attention away from the real reason she was there: to save her brother. Sometimes it would work, and she would get distracted and give up, but she kept getting back up and persevering.

Soon enough Sarah teamed up with some creatures she met in the maze: the coward goblin Hoggle, the beast Ludo and the knight Didymus and his dog Ambrosius. Together they saved her brother, and she woke up safely in her room where she first started. It was like it was all a bad dream.

This is exactly what happens when we follow Jesus. We get such high hopes in our journey. We have our Bible to lead the way, a positive attitude and our eyes fixed on Jesus. We start off knowing without a doubt that nothing can steer us away from following Him and making it to our destination.

How easy is it for us to somehow always change a straight yellow brick road into a labyrinth maze without an ending in sight? How easy is it for us to let the Goblin King, or Satan and his demons, distract us on our path and lead us in different ways? What happens when the storms of life come after us and swarm around us making us cower in fear? What happens when financial struggles come against us, and we don't know how we will pay the mortgage payment, and our home is being foreclosed? What happens when our child gets deathly ill, and nothing else in the world matters now besides being by that hospital bed, clutching our child's hand for dear life? When harmful memories of the past come swarming in demanding our attention and knocking us on the ground. When depression and mental illnesses cover our eyes and consume us with darkness. We can no longer see the light anymore. We can no longer see Jesus. We are lost.

I had high hopes. I wanted to follow Jesus no matter the cost. I took off running full speed and crashed to the ground confused on why I fell. I was weak and had nowhere to go. My ex fiancee left me with nothing when I left him. He allowed me to take my one suitcase of clothes and then allowed another woman to come in two weeks after and take my place being a mother to my child. I didn't have a job, and Mark took me off the bank account. I didn't even have money for a pack of diapers to buy for Adelynn! I didn't have a car because Mark had me sell that for extra money. Getting a job was hard because Mark would only agree in court papers to him having Adelynn in the daytime while he was off work and then me having her at night while he was working. Who would work with those hours? Heck, I would be on the streets if the church I attended hadn't given me a place to sleep.

I now know how my mom must have felt. And why she would constantly break out into tears and bring up me getting put into foster care. I get it now. I thought I never would, but I do.

I signed custody away. I'll never forget the day the judge asked me,

"Do you, Melissa, think this is in the child's best interest?"

I couldn't believe what I was doing. Tears ran down my face as I tried to force the words out,

"Yes, your honor...I do."

I walked out and couldn't hold it in any longer. I cried so hard. And not a little cry. It was an ugly cry. Everyone stared at me, but no one else mattered in that moment. The walk from the courtroom to the outside door felt like miles as I forced one foot in front of the other to leave. Run away. Get out. I felt like I was in a movie. Everything around me became blurry and in slow motion. This wasn't real.

I held onto faith that one day God would make this right. I had nothing else to lose, so I hoped that one day I would be there again, and this time leave that courtroom and fall to my knees in redemption and joy. One day things would get better.

I went to live with my mother and step dad in Florida to get myself together and save up enough money to provide for my children. Still holding onto the memory in my heart of experiencing God's existence, I didn't let these hard times get in the way of pursuing Him, getting back up after I let Satan knock me down.

I struggled to see God as the loving Father I read about. How can you understand something you've never experienced? One of the first books I purchased was *Abba Calling* by Charles Slagle. As soon as I read the first page, I knew I had to have it. It was a devotional. Every day was a letter from God, or Abba, to you.

If you are like me, in need of understanding God's love for you more, then this book is for you. I have never met this author. I am not marketing his book. It's fantastic. It's what helped me learn about this new experience. Learning about love. True love.

Because I had to know everything there was to know, I started reading at the beginning of the Bible. It took a while, but

I didn't stop until I was done. This is how God built a foundation in me that I would need for the road ahead.

JOURNAL ENTRY 5/21/13

How many more nights will I cry myself to sleep begging for your comfort? It seems I have every night I've been here. Come hold me, please, Daddy?
Melissa

I am not exaggerating. There wasn't a night I didn't cry myself to sleep. I missed my girls so much! It felt like a huge part of me was missing, and I was trying to find and put myself back together. I called the girls every day in the beginning, but I called less and less because the pain got worse and worse. I sent money every time I could, even if it meant splitting the check I got in half, and sending one half to each father. Mark tried his hardest to push me out of Adelynn's life, and with me being so far away, it was working. But no matter what I kept picking myself back up and trying desperately to get back to them. Just like Sarah in the Labyrinth.

JOURNAL ENTRY 5/22/13

Dear Daddy
I don't know how Mark can continue hurting me the way he is, doing everything he can to shove me out of my daughter's life like I never existed; like I never gave birth to her.
I forgive him Lord, and if there is something I haven't let go of yet, will you please take it from me? I'm starting to get discouraged and worn down. Please lift me up. Is it wrong for me to need from you so much? I can't help it sometimes. I've learned that you are the only one I can trust and the only one who can love me the right way. So now, with everything, I always come to You. I hope that's okay. I love you.
Love,
Melissa

Suddenly, memories of my childhood kept coming to mind, things I never remembered before. Sometimes when I heard people reminiscing about when they were a child, I thought it was all in their head because I couldn't remember much before age thirteen! So I researched it and learned about repressed memories:

Repressed memories are memories that have been unconsciously blocked due to the memory being associated with a high level of stress or trauma. The theory is that even though the individual cannot recall the memory, it may still be affecting them consciously, and that these memories can emerge later into the consciousness.

I am not sure why memories of my father came back after I became a Christian. Maybe God felt like I could handle it. Maybe it was time for healing. Either way, it was becoming more frequent and harder to deny.

Journal Entry 4/12/13

Dear Lord,

I stopped writing and I don't know how, but thoughts of my dad came into my mind. Sick thoughts. And I burst into tears. What is wrong with me, God? Why do I have those thoughts? Did my dad do those things to me, or is it all in my head? I hate this so much. I don't understand why I need to be tortured with thoughts like that. Will it ever stop? For so many years you have kept any memories of me being a child hidden. I don't understand why, if you were protecting me then, that you're not protecting my mind now? I'm sorry. I feel like it's me. Something's wrong with me. I wish I could fix it and it be over with now. I'll write more tomorrow. I want to lay down and read. I love you.

Love Always,

Melissa

One night I had a dream about it. Thankfully, it wasn't very detailed, but it was after my father had his way with me. He sat down on a chair still unclothed as he lit a cigarette,

"What do you think you're doing Liss?"

Even in the dream this confused me.

"What do you mean?"

He replied annoyed at the fact that I was even questioning.

"Your pastor? Being saved? Don't you know YOU'RE MINE!?"

I startled awake. I had no idea what this meant. But somehow I knew, deep down, that Satan was *mad*.

Sometimes flashbacks would come to mind. It was summer, and he took me to Disney World. I loved when he took me on trips like this! My grandparents on his side lived in Florida, and they would buy my father and me tickets to go to Disney World all the time. I loved roller coasters. Before I was tall enough to get on them, I begged my father for thick shoes and wore them under long jeans so you couldn't see. They made me tall enough to get on bigger rides. It was a blast, and there was something about the rush. My dad asked me if I wanted to get on some water rides, and I did! He said,

"All right, let's go change in the car and hurry back."

I jumped up and down and grabbed him by the hand, pulling him toward the car,

"Come on, Dad, let's go!"

We got to the car to change into our swimsuits. My dad had old shirts in the truck. He put them through the top of the cracked-open windows, which held them up there. The rest hung down to block the windows. There was a sun visor against the dash window and the back windows were darkly tinted, so we had complete privacy. At first I thought he was trying to give me somewhere to change into my bathing suit, but that changed when he turned his body in his seat so he was facing me. He smiled and stared at me, then shook his head in a way that almost said,

"Well, go ahead, take your clothes off."

I didn't want to. I was so scared in that moment. All the blood rushed to my face, and it was suddenly hot. Maybe I was sweating. A tapping noise on the outside window caught us off guard. My dad startled and shifted back into his seat, turning to roll down the window to see who it was.

It was a police officer. He asked why the windows were blocked.

"I was giving my daughter some privacy to change into her swimsuit, Officer."

The officer looked over at me, and I put my head down.

"Well, you can't block the windows. Take your daughter to the woman's restroom. She can change there."

God sent that police officer. I didn't know it then, but it was Him. He saved me from something worse. Maybe he scared my dad a little too because I can't recall anything happening after that.

My father was and still is heavily addicted to pills. They made him angry, and they have made him worse over the years. He was already angry to begin with, but the pills made it worse. He was controlling and dominant, abusive, cruel and hateful. Just being around him gave me a bad feeling in my gut. I don't know how to explain it. I always tried to make excuses for him, and he had a way of making it seem like I was the one with the problems, even crazy, and I believed it.

The next earliest memory I had of my dad, was him liking to be naked in front of me. I know up to a certain age it's innocent, but I was around ten years old. He put his hands on his hips and leaned his hips forward like he was showcasing his penis and wanted to make sure I was looking. I would quickly look away, and my face would get hot. I cannot physically recall my father ever raping me. Sometimes I try to remember, but I don't want to.

I thought there was something wrong with me. I held onto guilt and shame. It is hard to admit this part of my life, but dominant and submissive relationships intrigued me, and I became obsessed with researching this lifestyle. I thought it was what I needed. Someone to make me their pet, for me to become their possession. I didn't realize it then, but I was looking to fill a void with someone like my father. I wanted to *belong* to someone. I didn't know of any other way. I didn't know there was something better. I was lost in my labyrinth.

A friend of mine, Brian, brought up to me something about my father. We were at a birthday party I threw for one of my children. My dad was there following the kids around taking videos on his camcorder like usual. Brian and I had talked a few times about my memories of my father. Brian noticed the way my father was taking videos of all the children, and it freaked him out. He also brought up a time when he saw my dad drop me off to a cheer leading practice back in High School. He got the bad vibe even then. Brian shared his concern,

"You have to say something. I can't explain it, but I got this bad vibe seeing him with that camera. You know what's going on with you. What if it's happening to others too?"

I couldn't bear to imagine it. I could forget what happened with me, try to blame myself and push it under a rug, but I couldn't bare to think it was happening or has happened to others. I also realized that regardless of whether I remembered everything that happened, I couldn't allow him to be in my life anymore or around my children.

I told the police about the memories and that I had concern of it happening again to others. Because of the statues and limitations, they said,

"Can you go undercover to get him to admit this stuff? If you do, we could press charges, and we will call Social Services to check up on him."

I got my dad to meet me on-line through instant message to get his words in writing. I could barely talk to him over the phone without my voice stuttering, anyway. Before our meeting that night, an old friend who heard about the news I was coming forward with, Emily, messaged me. I hadn't heard from her in a while, and I was wondering why she reached out. Almost instantly, Emily confided in me that my father had also sexually abused her. She asked me why I was coming out with it now, and she said she tried to, but no one believed her, and she didn't think I would either. I got so sick in my stomach and angry inside. I apologized profusely for him and fell to my knees in painful cries. I know it wasn't my fault, but I felt so sorry and responsible somehow. She told me how when she came over looking for me and I wasn't home, he told her he wanted to play a game. He had them both stand in front of each other naked and look at each other. He told her it was a game that no one else could know. And she believed it, so no one knew for a long time.

I grew so angry inside. I was so angry for my father hurting her. He messed up her whole life in those moments! I asked myself why I didn't say something to anyone before about these suspicions. Then I remembered one night when I was talking to my father over the phone, and I asked him about this,

"Why can't you tell me you're sorry?"

He laughed with amusement. In his annoyed voice he said,

"Liss, there comes a point in your life when you decide if you're a victim or a survivor."

I remember him saying that all too well. It made me think I was crazy, and this was my fault. I went to a counselor about the abuse and told her those words he said to me. I needed someone to help me process it and gain the right perspective. As soon as I told her, she assured me that a man who was innocent, who truly and purely loved his child, would not say something like that when his child came to him with these types of things.

Even though it made me sick to my stomach, I still met him online that night. I got him to admit his sexual feelings for me now and in the past, but it wasn't enough. I had to have proof he sexually abused me as a child. I haven't spoken to my father since then. I know it scared him a little because he wrote me an e-mail trying to pin the abuse on someone else. I also know something changed that next day. The chains my father had on me weren't holding me any longer. Even getting through this chapter in my book about him, although I dreaded it, wasn't as hard as I thought it would be.

God has control of this situation, and ultimately, He is the judge. Out of this whole situation, you know what I've learned? It wasn't my fault, none of it. It wasn't my fault he was the way he was. It wasn't my fault I didn't know my worth and thought I was only worth enough to be someone's dog. It wasn't my fault he was stuck in that old house with no one to help him like he always complained about nearly every time I spoke to him. It wasn't my fault he hurt my friend Emily too. It wasn't my fault for any of it. Nothing. I am not guilty.

For so long I had misplaced shame and guilt. I know there is someone reading this that needs to hear those words. It isn't your fault, honey. We are neither victims nor survivors. We are overcomers. Let no one ever tell you different.

No matter what happened, how big or how small it may seem to you, it doesn't matter. It was wrong. It was sinful. Don't you let that devil hold you down with these chains any longer. There is a real God out there; He is your Father, and like He set me free, He wants to free you too. Please let him. It's NOT YOUR FAULT.

I thought this book was going to help others in similar walks of life, but with each part I finish, it's helping me too. Come and take my hand; there's more. Don't be afraid. I am with you every step of the way. We were never made to walk it alone. Let's walk this journey together so we can help each other find the ending to this labyrinth we made.

"Two are better than one, because they have a good return for their labor: If either of them falls down, one can help the other up" (Ecclesiastes 4:9-10).

four

DOUBT IN THE DESERT

*Nothing teaches us about the preciousness of the
Creator as much as when we learn the emptiness
of everything else.*
Charles H. Spurgeon

UNTITLED 12/30/2013

Watching the cars go by, they all have some-
   where to be.
I'm stuck on pause wondering, "Who is me?"
How did I get here to this place?
It's dark and cold and I keep thinking, "I got to
   finish this race."
The only place I run to is all the same.
Revolving doors, trying to remember my
   name.
Two names often come to mind they were
   formed in my womb.
I try to reach out to them in my dreams, but
   when I wake I'm back in front of my tomb.
Can I ever get back to hearing those songs I
   once sung?

Can anything breathe air back into my lungs?
Or will I sit and wait in these revolving doors?
Frozen like a statue hoping my legs will do
    more.
I wish I could take off full throttle
But then I give up and try looking at the
    bottom of a bottle.
But then there's two that come to mind and I
    know I need them soon.
Because you see they are pieces missing from
    me, formed right in my womb.

The morning sunshine peeks through the blinds in my window. It's dark in my room. Maybe my eyes are shut, I am not sure. I'm never ready to wake up. I hit the snooze button at least three times before I ever do. I am not sure why, but I take a while to want to get up. I am always tired. The first alarm goes off, and I hit it and then the second and a third until I know that if I don't get up now, I will be late. Late for what, I'm not sure.

One day when I got up, everything was different and the only memory I had was of the moment before. I fought to get back to Maryland to be with my children again. I fought to work two jobs to make enough money to rebuild our lives from the ground up. I fought to make others happy and let others make me feel worthless. I fought once again for love and acceptance from people in the world. I fought to find somewhere I belong. I fought hard...and then I gave up.

If I picture what it was like, I imagine Satan laughing while he told God,

"I told you so!"

He knew he had me now, and he brought back demons to torment me while I was down.

When an impure spirit comes out of a person, it goes through arid places seeking rest and does not find it. Then it says, 'I will return to the house I left.' When it arrives, it finds the house unoccupied, swept clean and put in order. Then it goes and takes with it seven other spirits more wicked than itself, and they go in and live there. And the final condition of that person is worse than the first (Matthew 12:43-45).

On those nights, I would drink almost an entire fifth of vodka. I got to the hotel room early to drink, so I was barely coherent by the time my "client" got there. He was there for one reason and one reason only, and the man who set them up for me always said,

"Make them happy."

I knew what to do. I knew what he meant. I have always been good at putting a smile on my face when I felt like I was dying inside.

I had given up trying to pretend like I would ever be somebody or ever make it in life. I wasn't worth any more than what my father said. I heard his voice in my head,

"You'll never amount to anything other than spreading your legs."

He was right. That's all I had to give, and my babies needed a bed to sleep on, food in their bellies and clothes on their back. In exchange, I took off my clothes, and I gave all I felt like I had to give. Me. Broken into pieces, but it was all I had to give.

I tried closing my eyes. I don't remember if I tried to think of other things. I was so empty and hopeless; I don't think there was anything else to think about. I let the alcohol take me over. How did I get here? How did I become numb to knowing right from wrong? Somebody shake me. I slept through my alarm. I know I did. This is a nightmare. It's not really happening. I've got to be still sleeping.

I doubted that this God, who first showed Himself to me as He did, cared about the torture it caused me to be separated from my kids. So I took it into my own hands. After I had enough money to purchase an old beat-up car, I moved back, and I tried hard to make it work. The path I chose landed me in places I didn't want to be in, with people I didn't want to be with, doing things I didn't want to be doing. I walked off without Jesus to walk this path by myself.

I wanted things to happen now. I needed time and money to be with my kids. The love of money became my stronghold.

The more I got, the more I needed. I tried to make excuses for myself and distract my thoughts by looking at all the things I was giving to my girls, being convinced that there aren't any other jobs that provide the same. Satan had won me over. I was at the point of no return. It was like I was on autopilot, and true thoughts and feelings were on silent, or even dead. I couldn't think or feel about what it was doing to me. Alcohol became my outlet and what I used to keep me from waking up and facing reality. It was too painful. I couldn't do it.

I think I tried to get out sometimes. Quickly, more hundred-dollar bills would be thrown in my face, and I got distracted and followed the money. I couldn't bring myself to leave.

How can I describe the dark place I was in to help you understand? Picture a girl with tear-and-black-make-up-stained eyes, stumbling all over the place, reeking of alcohol, crying in agonizing pain, feeling as if she was crazy and would pull her hair out. She doesn't run because she knows there is no way out. Now picture loud demons all around her, laughing at her and calling her names, pushing her and making her stumble, pulling her in every direction while they spit on her, hit her and kept her enslaved in chains in a deep, deep pit of darkness. That. That is the closest I can get.

The Bible talks about this same situation in Exodus. After the Israelites escaped Pharaoh and witnessed miracles and even God parting the Red Sea for them to walk across it, they had no reason to not believe in God. God freed them, and they should have followed Him no matter what because of all He had done for them. But they didn't. God got silent on them, and they doubted He would do anything else for them, or maybe they thought they had imagined what happened all along. They eventually led themselves into the wilderness where they stayed for forty years. They worshipped idols they could see and put their faith in them. Why? What makes us alike? Why do we doubt when God is silent or not moving things along on our timetables?

God doesn't work on our timetables. He has His own schedule. But most importantly, we lost faith. You see, the definition of faith is this:

Firm belief in something for which there is no proof.[2]

Proof? He showed us proof, didn't He? Well, maybe He did, but He hasn't for a while so maybe I imagined it. Maybe it isn't real. So instead of having faith in a God that I cannot see, I will put trust in this idol because I can see it, and it's real. I will trust these pieces of papers that can buy me anything I want. Right now that is my proof. That causes things to happen now. I can see it, and I need it.

I guess I lost faith. I guess I got tired of waiting and worried that the longer I wait, the more damage it will do to my children. If I could go back and change it all, would I? I wish. Then I would spare myself from all the emotional and mental damage. I'd stop debating whether I should reveal this part of my life to others because I'm afraid of how they will view me. I wouldn't think about the day my children eventually find out what I had done. I'd stop being worried about their response to it. Maybe...but what if it didn't?

I know God didn't cause this because only good comes from God, but if it happened, then He allowed it, and there must have been a good reason for it, right? What good could come from this? I wasn't ready to enter the Promised Land that God had for me. I didn't at all have the fruits of the Spirit that Galatians 5:22-23 tells us about:

But the fruit of the Spirit is love, joy, peace, forbearance, kindness, goodness, faithfulness, gentleness and self-control

I was depressed, angry and impatient. My heart was still filled with turmoil, and I had no self-control. I got to taste what it feels like experiencing God and His mercy, and then shortly after I got to experience what it feels like being in a deep dark pit with Satan. Maybe I needed that, to see what it's like with God or what it's like with the world. Maybe God was showing me that if I continue sleep-walking down my path, it will lead me to places like this, or I could wake up and choose His ways.

Whatever the reason for it, it needed to happen. The fruits of the flesh needed to die, and I needed drastic measures for that to happen. I didn't want this life. I remember how God

---

[2] "Faith." *Merriam-Webster.com*. Merriam-Webster, n.d. Web. 2 May. 2018.

showed Himself to me and the freedom I felt, and I wanted it back. So I searched for it. I ran away from people, places and things that would pull me back in another direction. I wasn't sure what to do, but I knew I had to work to make this better. I didn't want to ask Jesus for His help or to save me. I had gotten myself into this mess, and I would get out. I tried to save myself because I was too ashamed and too scared that I had disappointed Jesus.

Instead of hitting the snooze button over and over, I tried to get up. I searched for God and a way out of this darkness with all I had. I soon realized that the enemy wants me to sleep the day away, and he wants my eyes to be blind to the light shining through the blinds because the Bible says faith comes by hearing and hearing by the Word of God (Romans 10:17). If I am asleep, how can I hear? How can I seek if I am asleep?

So I opened my eyes and took off running. That's when I bumped into...Ronald.

five

TRIUMPHS TAKE TRIALS

*Not only so, but we also glory in our sufferings,
because we know that suffering produces
perseverance; perseverance, character; and
character, hope.*
Romans 5:3-4

Before I moved back to Maryland, I joined a dating website. It didn't take long for me to meet my husband, Ronald Smackhouse.

Ron and I had our first date in May. We took the children, my two girls and his son, to the beach. The date was horrible. I drove an hour to get there, and he didn't pay my way to get into the beach, which first got me thinking he wasn't the right one. When we left the beach, we planned to go to his house and order pizza for the kids, but instead he talked on the phone with his dad for an hour while the kids played at the park near his house. I realized he wasn't what I was looking for and made the excuse that I needed to take my girls home for bed to end the date.

Ron knew the date went bad. Later he asked me what he did wrong so he wouldn't do it with the next girl he dated, so I told him. We texted each other once in a while or sent Snap Chats to catch up for a few months.

By October we started texting a lot. We flirted and held long conversations. We gave another date a shot. He told me,

"I am in a much better place and not depressed like I used to be."

I no longer worked two jobs and had settled into my own home, so maybe this time it would work. We decided not to take our children this time. He said he would show me his gentleman side since I had been discouraged before.

Our date alone was in November 2014. I drove there on a Saturday. He took me out to a great dinner. Afterward, he took me down to the park by the beach. We walked by the water, and he kissed me and put his jacket around me to keep me warm. Then we went back to his house. The night before, he had mentioned me staying over because the drive was so long, and I had to get up early the next morning. I felt exhausted, so we lied down not long after. He put his arms around me and we both fell asleep.

We moved things along quickly. I wanted to come over one night and asked him which he prefers, "cheesecake or chocolate chip cookies?" He said,

"If you can make a good cheesecake, you might as well marry me now!"

I jokingly sent him a text saying I wore a size six ring.

Some nights he came to my house with his son Lawrence. He would spend the night and leave at 5:00 AM the next morning to get Lawrence on the bus and him to work. The talk of marriage came up again, but we questioned if it was too soon. We had dated other people in the past, and we knew what we were looking for, and each other was it. He said if we got married, we could live together and not have to worry about the drive. At the time, I had medical problems and needed a urologist, but I was self-pay and couldn't afford it. If we got married, he could put me on his insurance.

He proposed on December 5th, 2014. I was sick that day, and he had been caring for me. I fell asleep and woke up to him asking if I felt well enough to walk to the living room with him. He had candles lit, music going and roses laid out across the living room floor. Each rose had a little note, which said the reasons he loved me. He asked me to dance to a song he had playing on his phone. He got down on one knee and asked me to marry him, and I said yes.

We married the next week at the courthouse. We moved into his house to be closer to his work. I would find a job up there. Because of having to give my landlord a thirty-day notice, I gave it to her on December 29th and had thirty days after that to keep the keys. We got a four-bedroom house, instead of his two bedrooms, so each of our kids had their own room. It wasn't long until we were all moved into our new house and settled.

Things were rocky and stressful at first. It took two years to accumulate all I had for my children and me, and to gain independence, so not having a job made me nervous. My youngest daughter's dad, Mark, would criticize me for not financially providing enough for my kids, which always stuck with me. The talk of money stirred up a lot of arguments.

Some nights, because I still had my house I had rented before, I would go back there to get away from all the stress and feel like I still had a place to myself and I wasn't losing everything. He hated when I did this, and I understand why, but he didn't understand me or comfort me the way I needed; he only pushed me away. I wouldn't ever leave for too long, enough time to get my head together and calm down, and then I would come home.

When I started leaving during fights, Ronald thought something was going on to cause me to "run." I came home one night to find he had gone through my journals, which I had been keeping since April 2013. I started these journals addressed to God to show my journey with God and our walk together. I talked about everything in them, from my past, to what God was healing in me, to what I still needed healing from, and even where He showed up in my life. It was our whole journey together, and everything to be told was in them.

I walked in our front door and he was like a crazy person. He cornered me, flipping through my journals, asking me question after question, acting anxious, loud and upset about what he had read. One thing he asked was about how I admitted to God that sometimes I would use my body to get what I wanted because I felt like that was my only worth. He was furious with this. He said I "tricked" him into marrying me because I gave the perception that I was a single, strong mom who worked, was in school, and was a Sunday school teacher. I was all these things, but he said it was all a lie because I was nothing but the "whore" my journals admitted me to be. I had asked him if he wanted to know anything more about me before we got married and he said,

"Your past doesn't matter. All that matters is who you are today."

I took him for what he said and never thought about anything in my past. That was long gone, and I was a new person in Christ.

From this moment on, everything changed. It was like I met a different person. He changed from a gentle, loving man to a mean, horrible, anxious person, whom I did not recognize. He called me so many names, like "whore" and "cunt," mentally abusing me about my past all the time. He searched through my phone and yelled at me constantly. The littlest thing I did made him mad. I kept telling him I was sorry for my past, but that wasn't who I was today. He said it would not be easy to get over, but that he would try. I thought him acting this way was all my fault, and I felt bad, so I tried to endure all the mental abuse in hopes he would get past it someday.

A few times we talked about divorce. The first thing he would do is yank my rings off my fingers, saying he spent too much money on them and he wasn't going to waste it. Some nights he would say he was angry because I was supposed to be this "untouched, waiting for him, dainty woman," not who he read about in the journals.

One night I was getting ready to walk out the door because I couldn't take it anymore. I leaned up against the door with my head down crying while he yelled at me at the top of his lungs, calling me all sorts of names. His son walked by, and I saw him act as if this was nothing, like it didn't affect him. I remember thinking to myself, "If it was my kids, they would be so upset and terrified" because I never let them around these kinds of things. Whenever Ronald acted that way, I called my girl's dads to pick them up, or I would go drop them off, but his son acted like it wasn't anything new. It broke my heart because I tried to shield Lawrence from it too. That's when Ronald spit on me all over my face. No one had ever done that to me before; it was humiliating. I could smell his breath from the spit all over my face and hair. It hurt that he was that disgusted with me.

One time I checked in to a hotel room not far away. The lease to my house was already up. I tried calling my landlords to ask if they had already rented it in hopes to get it back, but they already had. Ronald had been trying to call me all night and the next day because he wanted me to sign a separation agreement. He wanted to make sure I didn't accumulate debt in his name, and he wanted to move on with someone else as soon as possible. I found out he took my rings back too. He was upset he didn't know where I was, and regrettably, I told him. When he got to the hotel, he convinced me to come back because he needed to know where I was and that we would talk about what to do next, so I went with him. We left my car there; he didn't trust me driving.

Back at the house, Ronald said he had talked to a lawyer, and I needed to stay until the next day to sign papers for the agreement. I didn't want this. I wanted so badly to be how we were before he hated me, when he used to love me, but I had no choice. He wanted it, and that was that. He had to go to work first, so he took my phone with him. I laid in the bed until he got back.

When he got home from work, he asked,

"If it was your perfect world what would you want?"

I cried,

"I want you to forgive me from my past and move on with me. Let's love each other and be together and stop all this fighting all the time."

That's when he told me what happened that day,

"I tried to get ahold of the lawyer all day, but for some odd reason, no one would answer at the office. I think it is a sign from God to stay and make this work."

So we tried again. He gave me back my phone, but told me

not to have a lock on it. I agreed. He took me to get my car, and I came home back with him.

He wanted me to change my phone number and stop talking to everyone I knew, including my mom.

"They will all be in your ear and might talk you into leaving, and it wouldn't help our relationship."

So I agreed because I wanted to make him happy no matter the cost. I changed my number and didn't give it a second thought. He looked through my phone a lot, and he wanted control over all my documents, like my social security card and birth certificate. I let him have it even though I found out he was keeping the same stuff from his ex-wives, which made me nervous, making me think,

"I am the next victim."

But I didn't dare pursue that argument with him.

Every day I was "walking on eggshells." I wanted to get a job so he wouldn't stress about money. I would pack his lunches and leave him little notes in there, trying to make him smile. I kept the house clean because he couldn't stand anything being out of place. I made him homemade meals every night. I tried to think of anything to make him happy.

One night I stood up for myself, and I immediately regretted it. I couldn't take the mental abuse anymore, so I said things like,

"Well, God doesn't say I am those things in my past. He says I am beautiful and holy in His eyes."

This angered him, and he yelled things like,

"Oh, holier than thou!"

That hurt because I never meant that I was better. I just meant I am worth something in God's eyes even if I wasn't in his. I said things like,

"God forgives me and doesn't hold me responsible."

And he would scream,

"I am NOT God!"

He took my things when I tried to get away from him. He would take my purse, keys, and phone and keep me where he wanted me. One night I tried leaving the bedroom to get away from him because I couldn't handle how bad he was bringing me down and questioning me over and over. He blocked me from doing so, and then when he had to use the bathroom, he grabbed me by the arm and dragged me with him so I couldn't get away. While he was using the bathroom, I tried loosening his grip on my arm. I tried closing the bathroom door on his arm because he was too strong for me. It must have stung his arm a little because he turned around while urinating and urinated on me. I thought it was an accident, but when he didn't stop and seeing the look in his eyes made me think otherwise. I'll never forget his face because he seemed like he liked it. I thought to myself,

"Why?" Why am I not worth anything more than the dirt on the ground for you to urinate on?"

Later that same night, after I showered and changed into clean clothes, it got worse. He was so angry at me for sticking up for myself. It was the first time he put his hands around my neck and strangled me. When he let go, I gasped to catch my breath and cried uncontrollably. I was so exhausted from trying to get him off of me and crying so hard that I laid down on the bed behind me. After he realized what he had done, he felt bad. He got into bed with me and held me while I cried myself to sleep. I told him,

"God will not continue to let you do these things to me forever. One day God will stand up for me."

I woke up the next morning when everything calmed down and told him,

"Ron, I thought you were going to kill me last night."

He tried to soothe me and said,

"No, baby I am so sorry. It was wrong. I should have never done it, and I promise I won't ever do it again."

As sickening as this is, I told him,

"It's okay. I deserved it."

I promised not to use it against him in future arguments and forgave him for it. It left bruises, so I covered it up with makeup so that at church on Sunday no one would see it. I told him it was okay because he showed remorse. I told him I won't even think about it, that he was the one bringing it up, and that I could forget it. He worried that I would not love him or treat him as well as I had been, but I told him that won't happen. I said as long as after he's done yelling, calling me names and whatever else, if he comes and holds me, calms down, and tells me he loves me, I would forgive him because I needed that reassurance that he still loved me when most of the time he didn't show it. I held on because I remembered the man he used to be. I missed that man and didn't want to give up, hoping he would be back to love me again.

In the midst of all this, I had been seeing a urologist since being diagnosed with interstitial cystitis. It's basically all the symptoms of a urinary tract infection, but without the actual infection. So I had the pain: burning, uncomfortableness, urgency feeling, and sometimes blood in my urine if the bladder wall was irritated enough. This made sexual intercourse painful at times. I took medicine called Hyophen three times a day to relieve some of the symptoms and make it easier to live with since it's an incurable sickness. Ronald was sexually active and admitted that before we got married, he planned to get a sex doll and he had a sex toy. He wanted sex all the time. I tried to give him what he wanted, but it made it hard sometimes because of my IC flare-ups. At first, I tried saying no if he wanted to have sex when I had a flare up, but he would say,

"You opened your legs to all these men in your journals, and you can't even do it for your own husband!"

He would tell me that being a submissive wife, like the Bible says, meant I couldn't have control over my own body, and I wasn't allowed to make those decisions. I believed him. So I tried to endure it. Either he was taking my pants off in the morning before I woke or he had to have it that night. Sometimes the pain was so bad, I begged him to stop,

"Please Ron, please it hurts, stop!"

He wouldn't ever stop until he was finished. On three different occasions, as soon as I got up, I ran to the bathroom in pain, sat on the toilet, and was so irritated that I urinated blood, crying on the toilet. Afterward, he said was sorry, that he hated seeing me in pain, but that was only after; he never stopped during sex except for one time. That one time he went in the bathroom for a while, so I knew what he was doing. I even asked him if he pleasured himself, and he admitted doing so. That made me feel like he didn't care about me at all. Only his pleasure mattered to him because that was his first concern, not that I was in pain.

As he had promised, he stopped physically abusing me for a while. Instead, he continued to take all of my things, my cell phone, purse, keys, and blocked me from leaving the room when we got into arguments. Some nights he wouldn't even let me sleep when I was exhausted. By this time I had gotten a full-time job, working Monday through Friday, 8:00AM—5:00PM as a call center specialist. After working all day, I would come home, hurry to clean the house, and make dinner for the family. I was also a college student online at Grace Bible College, pursuing my degree in human services for social work, so I had school work as well. My job required that I have the after-call phone with me some weeks, so my day never ended. I would be so exhausted that I begged him to let me sleep, but he wouldn't until we had sex.

The mental abuse in all this continued, and sometimes he would say things like,

"If we ever got a divorce, I will ruin you for the next man. You will never be able to love anyone else, and you will never stop thinking about me."

He also would tell me,

"Melissa if it's something that would make me mad or I wouldn't like, then you probably shouldn't be doing it. And if you do, you better tell me right away because when I find out, I will be madder at you for not telling me."

So this became my whole mentality. At one point I thought that I was going crazy because everything I did, everything I said, revolved around that comment. My thoughts anxiously became,

"Well, if I don't clean the house, he will get upset. If I say this or do this, he won't like it, and it will anger him, so I won't say it."

One time I lied to him, saying I had taken pictures of the bruises on my neck from when he strangled me because I needed him to know I would not let him do this to me forever. I wanted to show him that if I needed to stick up for myself, I would tell someone what he had done and continued to do to me. One night while I cried on the bathroom floor from him yelling at me again, he came in and said,

"Melissa even if you told, no one would believe you, anyway. Who will believe a girl with a broken past when I have a clean record and my career and you have nothing?"

He said if I told, he would make it so I would never get to see my children again. I believed him.

One day a friend of mine, Jordan, whom I have known since I was thirteen years old and have kept in contact with, e-mailed me because my number had changed. I e-mailed back from work. I told him I couldn't talk to him anymore, that my husband would be mad at me. At home I told Ronald what happened and never erased the messages because I thought of his comment. He said if something that would make him mad, I better tell him, so I did. He was furious! He e-mailed Jordan back and told him to stay away from me. Jordan is an attorney in North Carolina. He emailed Ron back and said,

"I prosecute men like you all the time! You are being controlling, and it is not right to control her that way."

But he never contacted me again.

I tried everything to make my husband happy. One time when I made dinner, he got upset that it was too early. One night when I spent too much time on my schoolwork, he got mad saying I didn't need to spend that much time on it. Every time I had my kids with us, he would tell me that I act as if they can do no wrong. He admitted to being jealous of my attention being on my children. I feared he might make me choose between them and him. He hated when I would have the after-hours phone and would make fun of me saying,

"I don't care about your stupid little cubicle job."

Nothing made him happy. It was never good enough. No matter how many times he put me down, I reacted with kindness, apologizing and telling him I loved him. At one point I said,

"Please Ronald, tell me what I have to do to make you happy, because nothing I do works."

I set up a date night for us to go to a Paint Night once, and that made him happy, but when we got back home, he was angry again.

We took a weekend getaway to New York. Ronald explained that it would help salvage our relationship, so I asked off for work. New York with him was amazing. I had my husband back! He was gentle and loving, pulling my chair out and helping me put my jacket back on. I grew hopeful again. When we were driving back, I got sad, and he asked,

"What's wrong?"

I put my head down and explained to him,

"I am scared that it will go back to how it was before. You aren't going to love me this much once we get home."

Ron worked for the government and he explained that he couldn't wait to get out of Maryland once he was transferred to another position. He didn't want to be reminded of all the memories of me going to a bar in town with a guy or whatever else bothered him. I thought,

"Am I going to go through this for the next who-knows-how-many years?"

I was right about him not being the same when we got back. He went back to the same old things. Fed up, I mentioned divorce, and he said he had already been e-mailing a lawyer about divorce, anyway. I wasn't sure what route to take, but I felt like any day now I would be at the end of my rope and would want out.

On the weekend of March 22, 2015 we took the children to the park down by the beach. I had brought kites to fly with the children, but it wasn't windy enough so they played on the park. Ron and I were sat on the bench arguing quietly so no one would hear us. I said he might need to see a doctor because his mood swings were too much. He snarled,

"I am not going to see a doctor!"

When he got irate, the first thing I would do is get my children back to their dads because I didn't like them around him when he acted that way. So I took advantage of being at the park in public and didn't get back in the car because I knew as soon as I did, he would take my phone, keys, and purse like he always did. I didn't know if I would have a chance to get my kids away. So I walked over with my kids and made the first phone call to Briley's dad, Frank. I called him and he wasn't surprised because I had called them many times to get the girls away from Ron. I told Frank where I was and that if I got back in the car, Ronald would take my phone. This made Ronald mad. He came over and snatched the phone from my hands, and it scared my oldest daughter Briley. She cried, and Frank heard it before Ron hung the phone up. I later found out that Frank had called the police.

Ronald gave my phone back, got the car seat out of the car, and drove away with his son Lawrence, leaving me and my two children there. A police officer came and said Frank had called them. He asked me if everything was all right. I said I was waiting for Frank to get there to pick up our daughter. He asked where I lived, and I told him with my husband up the road. He asked where he was, and I told him he left us here. I didn't say another word about what happened because Ronald always worried about something ruining his career with the government. I didn't want that for him no matter what happened with us, so I told the officer we were okay.

He left and Frank came not long after. My daughter has a dog she sleeps with every night that she can't sleep without, which we left at the house, so I called Ronald and asked him to bring it. He agreed. When he got there, I hadn't yet got ahold of my youngest daughter's father, Mark, so I agreed to go back in the car with him so my daughter and I weren't sitting out in the cold. I kept my purse with my keys and money in it close to my right side in the passenger seat so he couldn't take it. I had planned on running out of the car with my daughter and into my car as soon as we got home to get her out.

I thought of how he told me if I don't tell him something that happens, he would get madder, so I explained to him that Frank called the cops because he heard him yell and make Briley cry, but that I hadn't been the one to call. He got furious! I told him that I didn't tell them anything, that I sent them away, but he said,

"It doesn't matter, they are involved now. You're going to ruin my whole career!"

He then said,

"I will throw us all off this bridge right now and kill us all because my career is ruined!"

He swerved like he was going to do it while we were driving over the bridge. His son Lawrence, in the back seat, got scared, curled himself into a ball, laid down on the seat, covered his eyes and repeated over and over while crying,

"I'm scared, I'm scared."

I wished so bad that I could take him with me to safety, but I knew I couldn't, so I tried to console him and calm Ronald down at the same time.

We pulled into our neighborhood and Lawrence, still crying, asked to get out of the car and go play with his friends. Ron let him. I was happy for that. At least he was away from his dad for a little while. I saw Mrs. Jacobs, our next-door neighbor, outside with her daughter, so I took the opportunity to get my daughter and I in my car and get out of there. We got into the car and drove away. I couldn't get a hold still of Adelynn's father, so I got her some lunch while we waited.

Ronald kept calling me, and a couple times I answered. He said he talked to someone to find out how to protect himself from getting in trouble. He said he was getting an order to make me stay away from the house. He said not to come back there, that he kicked us out. He told me he planned to leave town.

I got ahold of Mark, my daughter's father, and drove to his house to explain the situation. He told me he couldn't take Addy. He had to be at work tomorrow, and he couldn't miss it and had no one to babysit. I asked him what he wanted me to do because Ron had kicked us out, and he told me to call Social Services because he wasn't allowed to kick us out. So I did. After hearing the situation, a woman from Social Services told me I needed to call CPS because of his threat to kill us and the kids being involved. We made a three-way call to them, but it went to an answering machine. She called the domestic violence shelter and connected me with an advocate there, Danielle. Danielle put my daughter and I in a room for the night. She told me she would be there later that night to talk.

I realized that I would have to tell what my husband had been doing to me. I wanted to believe that my husband and I could make things work, so I called him. I told him I would talk to someone later that night, and I would have to tell them everything he had done to me. I asked if there was some way to make this work because I didn't want to report him. We talked about marriage counseling and he begged me to come home. He would Lawrence to his mom's house then he turned around and come home.

I contemplated it and decided to give it one more shot. I loved my husband and wanted him to love me and make this work. Addy and I got back to the house at 12:30 or 1:00 AM on Saturday that weekend. He settled down and went to bed. I took Addy to her room, and she was upset, so I sang her a few songs until she fell asleep. Then I fell asleep in my oldest daughter's bedroom.

Danielle, the advocate from the shelter, texted me. I had my phone with me because I told Ron that if he took it, the people that have been trying to reach me might get worried that he abused or abducted me again, so he let me keep it. I didn't answer her yet because I wanted to make sure he didn't do anything to me and that he wasn't saying we would go to marriage counseling as a trick. Social Services tried calling me back as well and left a message. He said I needed to text and call them back and tell them we are fine now and going to marriage counseling. I said I would in the morning because I didn't know what to say to them. He said if I told the truth, he wouldn't be able to look at me and love me anymore. This made me sad because I only wanted him to love me. He told me he wished I would choke and die because he didn't like me having the control of telling on him and having my phone to do so, and it would be an easy way out of the marriage.

I brought Addy to her dad after work around 4:30 PM that Sunday and then came home. We didn't have any children with us as we usually do, so we had a couple drinks to talk about where to go from here and relax. I admitted to him that I got a pack of cigarettes to help calm my nerves. He hated that I got them, as I had quit a while ago, and got angry with me. He told me he didn't like seeing something have control over me. He poured the bottle of alcohol down the kitchen sink because he didn't want that to have control over me either. He got angrier.

I was exhausted in every way. I wanted to go to bed. This made him angrier. He dragged me to the shower and made me take my clothes off. He turned the cold water on and made me get in and stand in it. I stood at the end of the shower, trying to cover myself while crying and wondering,

"Why? Why does he hate me so much? Why is he doing this to me? What did I do to make him so angry?"

He let me get out. I dried off, and he picked out pajamas for me, my pink polka-dot ones. I laid down while he got my pants on, and he continued to yell at me and get angrier. I said nothing in fear that anything I said would make it worse, so I kept my mouth shut. This made him angrier. He got on top of me and hit me across the face. I remember hearing like he might have slapped me the first time because it made a noise against my ear like something had hit it. Then I felt a closed-handed fist twice more as my head went back and forth. I kept my eyes shut tightly to brace myself, afraid to see what he might do next. He had never hit me like that before, so I was terrified.

After he got off of me, I went into survival mode. The closest thing to me was the window in the bedroom, so I ran over to it hoping it would be unlocked or I could bang on it and someone outside would hear me. He came behind me and swooped his arm around my waist, knocking me down. I had held onto the blinds and pulled them down with me. He got on top of me and put one hand over my nose and mouth and the other around my neck. I remember thinking to myself,

"I am going to die. I am going to die! This is it for me! Jesus, please help me!"

I closed my eyes, because I didn't want the last thing I saw before I died be that look in his eyes. I couldn't move my legs, but my hands were free. With my eyes shut, I put my hands up hoping to feel for skin, doing anything to get him off of me. I started clawing at his face and at one point I got my mouth open and bit his finger. He got off of me, and I quickly crawled to the bathroom. He kept telling me over and over,

"Look what you did to my face!"

I saw him pull out his phone, and I saw the camera app opened, and I wondered what he was doing. He put his phone up as if to record me. I cried on the bathroom floor, gasping for breath in shock and confusion. He kept telling me,

"Admit it! Admit what you did to me!"

I cried and cried. He walked out of the bathroom, so I got up and ran towards the front door in hopes to get out. He came behind me, leaned up against the door and held it shut. I banged on the glass panel beside the front door and yelled for help. He kept shaking his head saying,

"No, I'm going to tell what you did to me. I'm not going down for this."

He ran out the door, and I saw him run to the left towards the Jacobs' house.

The police showed up not long after. I tried explaining to them what happened, that he had strangled and hit me, and it all started because we were talking about a divorce. They shined a flashlight on my neck and because they didn't see anything, I guess they didn't believe me. They arrested me. I later found out they arrested us both because they couldn't determine who the aggressor was.

What happened after all this is another story entirely. Today I am pursuing charges against Ronald for strangulation, rape, assault, and abduction.

six

RESURRECTION

*You were taught, with regard to your former way
of life, to put off your old self, which is being
corrupted by its deceitful desires; to be made
new in the attitude of your minds; and to put
on the new self, created to be like God in true
righteousness and holiness.*
Ephesians 4:22-24

*When we come to the end of ourselves, we come
to the beginning of God.*
Billy Graham

I spent two nights in jail. All the bruises, from head to toe, appeared the next morning. A policeman there saw them and seemed to have a look of guilt on his face as he nervously said,
"Oh...you did get beat up, huh?"
When the time came for my bail hearing, my husband walked into the courtroom dressed nice with his lawyer, while a police officer escorted me in an orange jumpsuit and handcuffs. I came up to the judge and pleaded with tears in my eyes,
"Please, your Honor...I shouldn't be here. I have been trying to tell everyone here to listen to me, but no one will. I need to

get out so I can get ahold of my advocate, Danielle, from the Abused Women's Shelter. She knows about this whole situation. I have no one to come bail me out because my husband had me stop talking to everyone. I have an employer probably wondering where I am, and I need to tell them what happened because that job is the only thing I have left now."

Ronald's lawyer asked for a protective order, and the Judge scoffed at him,

"Like you really need protection from her!"

The judge let me go free. I called Danielle and explained what happened, and she got on the phone with a police officer there and convinced him to take me to the shelter since I had no ride and no money to take myself. As soon as I got there and they saw me, Danielle took me to the hospital. She said people have died days later from strangulation, and she wanted to get me checked out to make sure I was okay.

The doctors and nurses rushed in to examine me and take pictures. I had another moment where I felt myself fading from the realization of things going on around me. How did I end up here? I remember praying one night in my head while in the room at the shelter with my other roommates, and saying with a deep, heart wrenching, silent cry,

"God, I am losing faith. Did I imagine what happened? How could you let this happen to me? I thought You loved me."

I am brought to tears even now as I type this because I remember that feeling so well. I am not sure I could hurt more than in that moment.

The last chapter you read was excerpts of the exact letter I turned into the prosecutor's office after they let me out of jail. My victim witness told me to spend the evening writing every single detail of how we met, how we got married and everything that happened after that, to turn in to the police. She said he couldn't try to lie his way out because there will be too many details for him to lie about, and he will trip himself up. So I went back to the shelter and started from the beginning, writing every detail.

Everything that happened from there felt like a spiral whirlwind heading straight for Hell. I had to re-live the story over and over again. Every day I had numerous calls from new people wanting to hear my side of the story. Yesterday it was this prosecutor, to this lawyer, and today it's this advocate and this victim witness. It was never-ending. I got diagnosed with PTSD and put on anxiety medicine because I couldn't sleep at night. I thought he would come after me because I thought he would kill me if I ever told. I had a protection order against him, but no one understood me when I cried saying,

"It's a piece of paper! What am I going to do with this when he comes to kill me, throw it at him?"

My roommates told me I cried every night in my sleep when I dozed off from the medicine. I had nightmares all the time. Every time I saw a silver Mazda that looked like his car, I had a panic attack. I researched how to get a will and life insurance so that my girls would be okay if anything happened to me. It messed me up. I thought the comment he made about ruining me for the next man was true! I felt ruined. I talked to my mother on the phone shortly after, and she wasn't surprised at my story. She knew he was like that the moment he married me without telling anyone. I cried telling her what he said,

"Mom! It's true! He did ruin me. This is it for me."

She had her strong, reassuring Mom voice,

"No Liss! Don't you dare listen to that. He didn't ruin you; he only made you stronger!"

I tried to keep the faith. I don't know why. I hoped there was something better than this. I still attended church, wanting to be strong for my girls and not let them see my weakness. One night my youngest daughter Adelynn spent the night with me. It was the weekend, and we got up the next morning to get ready for church. All the women at the shelter were so nice. There were other little kids Adelynn's age, and they were outside in the fenced-in swing set, laughing and playing as I rushed to get ready to leave. I felt my phone keep going off. I always have it on silent so it vibrates. It annoyed me as I hurriedly tried to finish getting ready. I looked, and it was my sister in Michigan calling. By the time I looked she must have called four times, so I knew something was up. I called her back,

"What's up Susan? I'm getting ready for church."

She was in hysteria, and I almost thought she was drunk.

"Did you hear, Melissa?! Oh my God! Mom's dead!"

I didn't believe her. I couldn't; she was lying!

"No, no, no, it's not true, I don't believe you! NO!" I lost grip of the phone to my ear and it crashed to the ground. I fell to my knees and screamed in agonizing pain. I rocked back and forth with my head in my hands, crying out,

"Noooooooo! Noooooo!"

I knew the constant popping of her pain pills wasn't right, but I honestly thought she was handling it. She had been diagnosed with Hepatitis C a while ago and had been on Vicodin and Valium ever since. Everyone got used to her always being on them. She had built up a tolerance for it, and she was my mother, and I thought she would take care using them. I don't know what I thought. Maybe I got so used to everyone in the family being dysfunctional, including myself, that it was nothing new. That's what you always think when you face something like that, right? That it will never happen to you. Well, I was wrong. It can happen and it did.

I drove from the shelter to Florida to help my step-dad with the funeral arrangements. I drove all night, straight through. I stopped a few times at a rest stop to collect myself. I was so angry at God. I shook my fists to the night sky,

"How could you? How could you? After everything I have been through, you take my mother away when I need her the most?"

I didn't say it, but I felt at that moment that I hated God. I was so angry at Him. How could He let this happen when I kept holding onto faith and picked myself back up? After I got all of my anger out on the nearly seventeen-hour drive, I came to some acceptance. God and I weren't on the best terms, but I stopped being so angry with Him and prepared myself for the family drama to come.

It didn't take long for things to spiral down in my family after Mom died. Everyone wanted to blame someone, and they blamed me because my siblings said,

"You're the reason Mom was so unhappy!"

I can't blame them. Maybe I was. I know that I didn't mean to be, but I do know that me getting put into foster care haunted Mom, and she was overwhelmed with guilt. Sometimes she would bring it up, crying and apologizing, and I would try to console her and tell her it needed to happen. I never held grudges and once I was saved, I realized how broken we all are in this world. It made me view my mother in a new way, like I wasn't the child anymore, but more like a mother to her. Either way, no matter who is to blame, my mom was gone. And that was that.

She was laying on the couch in the living room. Next to her was a piece of crust from a pizza she had eaten before she went to sleep. She always slept on the couch and ate a lot at night since she didn't eat during the day. She said it made her tired. The autopsy said she died in her sleep from Morphine. At least she was sleeping when it happened. That was one of the many things I told myself to bring some light into the dark place I was in.

Her funeral was sad. Some Episcopal pastor who didn't even know our family said a few words. My sister Susan was late, drunk and dramatic. There was a lot of hostility in the room and the tension could be felt. They cremated my mother and put her into a grave in Michigan close to her family. I got up after the pastor and read a poem I had written in case no one else said anything.

FOR MAMA 5/3/15

This child had a purpose although she never
knew.
She was living it all along, by loving all of you.
Protection for her children and to love her
mother strong.
Her will unbreakable, her love so fierce, and
she always thought she got it wrong.
So deep it this type of love to sacrifice all
things,
The angels would look down smiling, over her
they would sing.

> You see, she never left defeated, it was
> redemption she had won.
> She persevered and fought the good fight and
> now her battle is all done.
> Although you are in sorrow, this was not a
> waste.
> My child has crossed the finish line, she finally
> won the race.
> I gently came to her and whispered in her ear,
> "Darling, come home to Me." She smiled and
> there was no more fear.
> I held every tear she cried and wiped them
> from her eyes. I clothed her in pure white
> and crowned her with glory
> I made sure she knew her worth and she loves
> to hear that story.
> She may seem far from you, but children listen
> when I say,
> "You will see your beloved again when I come
> back for you on our coming home day."

I brought my guitar with me. I learned to play while I was living with my mother in 2014. She had a guitar sitting in a case, untouched. I asked her about it one day. She shrugged,

"I bought this guitar when you were a baby. I was going to teach myself to play, but I never got around to it."

I taught myself to play on that very same guitar. I always loved that story and tell it every chance I get. The first song I learned to play was "Over You" by Miranda Lambert. Mama used to love hearing me sing and play that. Her dad died shortly after I learned it, and she had me play it for him at his grave as tears ran down her cheeks. I sang and played that song one last time before they lowered Mom's ashes into the ground.

Back in Maryland, things got worse. Nothing made sense anymore. Everything going on with my husband was chaotic, and the anxiety got worse. I went on an alcohol and drug binge. I tried heroin a few times and overdosed twice. I was brought back to life in the hospital with a black eye and no recollection of how I got there. I didn't care, and to be honest, I wanted more heroin so I could nod back out. It was easier for me to be passed out than to be awake and deal with things. I wasn't working, but I received spousal support that my husband was ordered to pay. I got out of the shelter and into a trailer not too far away. I wanted to die. My mom dying was the absolute last bullet to my heart, which I knew had killed me.

I am not sure what brought me to my knees again that night. I was drunk and alone inside my trailer. I didn't want this life of drinking and drugs, but I didn't see myself getting out of it. I had nothing to live for except my children, but I thought I wasn't a good mother for them either. I fell to my knees in agonizing turmoil and pain in my heart, and I yelled out,

"God! I can't do this! I can't get out of this cycle! I can't help myself! Please help me because I can't anymore, Please help me."

I had gone to a group called Celebrate Recovery for the first time in Florida when I was living with my mother. Celebrate Recovery is like Narcotics Anonymous, but it is Christ-centered. It's not just for drugs and alcohol, but their saying is that it's for "Hurts, Habits and Hang-ups." I needed help with all those things. I knew of one in the area so I went. I had nothing to lose. I remember sitting in the church pew when the leader had finished the lesson for the night. They were calling people up for chips. One chip for years in victory over whatever they had originally gotten the first chip for, one for six months, three months, and one month. I saw someone go up for their thirty days chip and thought to myself,

"Thirty days clean...I wish I could see that."

I knew I never would, but I couldn't help imagining it. As I write this to you today, I want you to know I have seen so many chips since then. Some I thought I never would. It didn't happen overnight. That silent thought was a prayer and hope I didn't know I was even asking for, but it was answered. I never touched heroin again. I drank alcohol less and less. That moment was a turning point for me. I ended up speaking my testimony for the first time in the very same Celebrate Recovery group. It's where I started my first Step Study Classes. A miracle I couldn't see or feel happened that night.

I moved closer to where I had lived before I got married. The PTSD hadn't completely gone away, but it subsided little by little. I tried to be strong all day for my girls. After I put them to bed, I would go in the shower and fall to my knees and cry so hard until I got tired. I didn't see it then, but I was healing and those tears were needed in that process. I got a job and my girls and I rented a two-bedroom apartment. It wasn't much, but it was ours. It was in a cornfield and I loved the country views and the freedom it gave me. I would often go outside at sunset and talk to God while I watched the colors change in the sky. I was making it. Things were getting better and maybe my mother was right. I wasn't ruined. I was stronger.

"I Am" 2015

Yesterday I made dinner too early, you didn't like it
I am such a screw-up.
Yesterday you spit in my face, I don't deserve respect
I am unworthy
Yesterday you put me in a choke hold, I deserved it
I am out of line.
Yesterday I realized everything I do to try and make you happy isn't good enough
I am a failure
Yesterday you peed on me in disgust while I cried
I am the dirt on the ground
Yesterday I tried to get away and leave you, you took my keys and money
I am a prisoner
Yesterday you told me if I ever left you, you would make sure I was ruined first

I am damaged

Yesterday you told me if I get wrinkles like
my mom, you wouldn't love me anymore

I am ugly

Yesterday you made fun of my job, I told you
one day I would get something you would
be proud of

I am unimportant

Yesterday you called me horrible names

I am what you say

Yesterday you told me to change my number
and not talk to even my mother

I am controlled

Yesterday you told me I am not allowed to
leave the house

I am isolated

Yesterday you had your way with me even
though I cried and begged you to stop,
you said I wasn't allowed to say no

I am your possession

Yesterday you wouldn't let me sleep until you
were done yelling at me

I am tired

Yesterday you turned the cold water on and
made me get into the shower

I am humiliated

Yesterday you hit me three times across the
face

I am a victim

Yesterday you held me on the ground and
strangled me

I am going to die

Today I am in the hospital while they count
my wounds and take pictures of my body

I am exposed

Today I am trying to learn how to live without your control

I am dependent

Today I am hiding from you in a shelter
I am afraid
Today I had a panic attack and was told I had
    PTSD
I am diagnosed
Today I cried in my sleep
I am still healing
Now I am smiling again
I am hopeful
Now I am accepting the truth God says about
    me
I am worthy
Now I am no longer a victim
I am a survivor
Now the nightmares have subsided
I am an overcomer
Now I am gaining self esteem
I am beautiful
Now I am providing for myself
I am independent
Now I believe that my mom was right, I am
    not ruined
I am stronger
Now I am able to let go and forgive you
I am merciful
Now I am leaving the chains behind me
I am free
Yesterday I belonged to you, Today God has
    set me free, and now I am His

One day I sat outside after an interview I had that morning. I wanted this job. It was salary paying, had great benefits, a small office and doing something I am good at, and the company even had fun family activities every year. I knew my girls would love that. After praying again for it, I looked at my missed calls and saw one from a prosecutor to charge my husband with felony charges. As I put the phone back down to think about what I would say to her before I called her back, I asked myself,

"What would Jesus do?"

I immediately got a vision in my head of him telling the woman everyone wanted to stone cause she had committed adultery,

"Go, and sin no more."

I imagined saying that to Ronald would somehow bring him to his knees and help save him because he would see the mercy of God as I showed him God's grace. As much as I wanted to hate this man for everything he did, I couldn't go through with charging him and sending him to jail. I called her back and told her of my decision, and she asked me why.

"It's not my job to punish him. God is the Judge."

That was that. I dropped all charges. I was still on his health insurance, but agreed to end the spousal support, and I knew God would take care of us financially. Time passed and things got easier. It was almost like the tornado that had come into my life and destroyed everything and lasted so long was over. Now everything was being renewed and restored.

FORGIVENESS LETTER TO RONALD
12/23/2016

Dear Ronald,

I am not sure if this letter will even make its way to you or if it's really you reading this letter. Nonetheless, I am writing regardless. Before I have my closure, there are things I need to say to you, not seeking a response.

I am sure you probably think this letter will be spiteful, but I assure you it's not. I don't have room in my heart for spite. This letter is for closure, and it's also to thank you.

In the beginning I was so angry with you. It took lying on the floor in the jail to realize that you not only put me there, but you did it knowing you were wrong, and you didn't care about me, only yourself. Before I even told anyone about the bruises you had left all over my body, I cried. I didn't want to do it. Even after all that, I still tried to protect you.

One of the last things I said to my mother before she passed away was,

"He was right, Mom. He did ruin me."

Remember saying that to me—that you were going to ruin me for the next guy? Well, you almost succeeded because that was the last attack to my heart that I could take. I felt like giving up for sure. But you know what she said ?

She said, "No Liss, he didn't ruin you. He made you stronger."

And you did. So for that I have to thank you. She was right. I wasn't ruined or broken or damaged. I was stronger and made new. What I thought would kill me emotionally and mentally only made me more of the woman I am today. And I love that woman. She is strong and mighty and fierce, and she is a loved child of God.

I had to remember who I was and who Jesus was. I pictured Him looking at you and saying,

"Go Child, and sin no more."

So I put that rock down and forgave you. Even if you're not sorry and you still feel this was my fault, it doesn't matter because I forgive you, anyway. If I can forgive someone who wasn't even sorry, my mom was right, that's strength.

I called the prosecutor on the case and asked that everything be dropped: the investigation, any charges, everything. I also remember once when you said you wanted to experience God the way I have. Well, I thought this was for you. You witnessed Him firsthand through me. Mercy and grace, even if you don't feel like it, was extended to you. Trust me, it was. Unfortunately, they still let you go from your job. That was out of my hands, but it could have been worse.

I don't know what the future holds for you. I pray for you, and I hope this was an eye-opener. I hope and pray this won't happen to someone else. You have a lot of anger in your heart that you need healed. I know there is good in you. Maybe something happened in your past to give you insecurities, and I hope you find freedom from that.

I want to thank you also for my future. If it wasn't for you, I wouldn't have become the stronger woman I am today. If it wasn't for you, I wouldn't have been able to appreciate even more the man I have in my life. Sometimes to appreciate your dream, you have to live through your nightmare first. You helped show me how strong I am, and for that I thank you.

If it wasn't for you, I wouldn't have had such a strong testimony that had an impact on so many people. The Chief of Police came up to me afterwards and said he's seen and heard it all, and people with my story never make it. The fact that I did astounded him, and he said I could help so many girls like me. I used to be so afraid of telling people about my past because of how you made me feel about it. You made me feel like I deserved to be punished and I wasn't forgiven. But I stepped out in front of a crowd of people and told them the truth. I was scared of how they would see me, but instead of judging me like I thought they might do, I had a standing ovation. People cried out because my story touched their lives so much, they wanted the Jesus they saw in me.

Ronald, you gave me something through all this. You gave me freedom. I was stuck inside a prison I made for myself, thinking I would be judged by my past. It wasn't only you who made me feel that way. I did it to myself too. God promises to turn all things into good for those who love Him. He used even this, and He did just that.

So thank you. I forgive you; I know you don't know what you were doing. I truly hope and pray things get better for you and you get the healing you need. And Ronald, I am sorry too. I truly, deeply mean that.

Goodbye Ronald,

Liss

Healing took place over time. One by one the broken pieces of my heart mended. It's funny how as soon as I forgave Ronald and dropped the charges against him, it felt freeing for me and things changed for the better.

Maybe that's why the devil became afraid and tried to use different ammo on me. Not long after I started having some health issues going on, nothing drastic, but I had it checked out. By accident, trying to check for something else, the doctors had found something. I had a brain tumor. It was non-cancerous, but had grown large and needed to be immediately removed. I sat in my Neurology Surgeon's office while he told me about the procedure and what to expect.

"Just like with any surgery, there are death risks, so we will need you to sign a permission form. We will have to shave your hair on the right side and make an incision behind your ear. Where the tumor is positioned, we will cut through your ear canal, and unfortunately, you will lose all hearing in the right ear. I intend to get it all out, but this will be a long procedure. It is wrapped around your facial nerve and will take caution to get to. We might need to cut through your facial nerve if we are unsuccessful getting it. You will lose all function in the right of your face, but don't worry, you can have plastic surgery to get it fixed."

I am not sure what all he said after this. Here I was once again drifting off into my head. Wrapping my thoughts around what was happening. At this point I had gotten used to bad things happening and so this didn't have an effect on me like it should. I wasn't afraid of the tumor or surgery and I am sure my fearlessness made Satan even more fearful. The only thing I can remember thinking about is, that I didn't want to do it alone. I had already been through so much alone and I couldn't do it anymore. So I prayed,

"God please. I know you are always with me and that should be enough, but God please I cannot do this alone. Please send me someone who will love me the way you do here on earth so that I may understand the love you have for me because I don't feel it."

It wasn't long after I left my Neurosurgeon's office that I was back at the hospital prepping for my Ten-hour long surgery. I was changed into a gown laying in the roll away hospital bed when a doctor came in and signed his initials with a permanent marker behind my ear where they would make the incision. The rolled me away into the surgery room and all the doctors and nurses were waiting with masks over their mouths. They had on gowns and gloves and machines were everywhere beeping. They had a mask waiting for me to put around my mouth to inhale the anesthesia to put me to sleep. The doctors slipped the mask over my head and onto my mouth. Not even two breaths in and I shut my eyes, not knowing if I would wake or if I did, what to expect next.

seven

REDEEMED

But now, this is what the Lord says--he who
created you, Jacob, he who formed you, Israel:
"Do not fear, for I have redeemed you; I have
summoned you by name; you are mine."
Isaiah 43:1

Then I will make up to you for the years
that the swarming locust has eaten.
-Joel 2:25

I have learned that sometimes God waits for something in you to die so that He can bring something better to life.

I slowly opened my eyes...where was I? How long had it been, and what happened? Then I noticed the throbbing pain in my head. I was in a hospital bed and had woke up from surgery. I heard a soft, gentle voice, and I looked up. He had a relieved but still worried look on his face,

"Hey baby... How are you? Everything's okay. You're awake. I was so worried, babe."

Wait, he wasn't a dream? He was real? I didn't imagine him, but here he was praying and waiting for me to open my eyes.

I remembered when I first met him. It wasn't long before the surgery. I wasn't working at the time, and I had my two girls to support. We rented an apartment that I could barely afford, and I had spent the last of my income tax refund. I was so worried to let my girls down again and lose everything we had worked hard to get. So I swallowed my pride for once in my life, and I asked for help. I wrote a post on my church Facebook page:

"My name is Melissa. I am a member of our church. I don't ever ask for help, but I decided to see if there was anything I could do. I try to figure everything out by myself and have always been too afraid to ask for help.

I am a single mother of two kids and am about to have brain surgery. It's hard to find a job that will hire me knowing I will be out for a couple months for recovery.

I need to make the rent payments and afford to feed my children. I am not asking for handouts; I am willing to do work. I have cleaned condos by the beach before. Just any side jobs to work for the money, or even if anyone knows anyone that would hire me. It would be a big help. Thank you."

Not even five minutes after I posted that, I got a message from someone named Rob asking me to clean his house. He told me he couldn't afford it all the time, but he wanted to help me out if I came this weekend. I was overwhelmed by how many people reached out and wanted to help. Some people gave me jobs. Some had been through a similar surgery and wanted to be an ear or help my family. I was in awe. I still felt out of my comfort zone, but I didn't want to only do things the way I knew. I wanted God's ways.

God had taken that pride I held on to and used it to open doors I never thought I would see. I trusted Him financially, and He provided.

I knocked on the door of my first house to clean with a mop and bucket filled with cleaning supplies in my hand. Rob opened the door, and he had a surprised look on his face,

"Melissa?"

I wasn't sure how to read it, and maybe he didn't realize that the girl he responded to was the same age as he was.

Maybe he thought I was older.

"Yes, that's me."

His mood lightened. "Oh, okay. Well, I'll be going in and out to my dad's house across the street. Feel free to use my cleaning supplies. They are over there under the sink." He pointed to the right in the kitchen.

"All right, thank you. I brought all my own though. I used to clean for a living."

I quickly got to work.

His house didn't seem very dirty for a man, but I noticed boxes still packed. He had recently moved in. It was beautiful and spacious, and my favorite part was the backyard that had so much land. I didn't see any ring or notice anything that belonged to a woman in the home, but I tried to dismiss those thoughts from my head. What was I doing? I was there to clean. I put my iPod in my ears and worked.

When I finished and had put my things back in my car, I turned back inside for one more thing. He had come back from his dad's and stood in the kitchen waiting for me,

"How much do I owe you?"

I didn't want to charge him like they do at the condos by the beach, and I wasn't sure how much to charge.

"Just whatever you feel lead in your heart to give. Nothing is too small. Anything will help"

Little did I know that one day soon, that house would become my home. Cleaning that house after the first time became a regular thing for me.

Rob and I dated shortly after, and we have been inseparable ever since. I tried to push him away. I thought no one would be attracted to me after my face was messed up from surgery, but he never budged. He was sent right in time because honestly, I am unsure how I would have made it by myself after surgery.

But I opened my eyes and he was still there. Everyone in my life always told me to suck it up, that it wasn't that bad. But Rob never complained or got irritated with me. It hurt to walk again, and he held me up to walk every time. My balance was off, so sometimes he would carry me. I can't praise this man enough for all he did and got me through. There aren't any words, and I am still trying to comprehend it all. One thing I know is that God answered that prayer I made.

Rob was the first man in my life who didn't yell at me or criticize my past and wrongdoings. As soon as it started getting serious, I made him watch my testimony that someone had recorded for me the first time I spoke it. I wanted him to know the whole truth about me, whether he said he cared to hear it or not, so that nothing surprised him later. If after seeing it, he didn't want to continue dating me, I was okay with that. I would rather have been single than to ever go back down a road similar to what my ex-husband, Ronald, put me through. After I got done showing him, fully expecting him to want to leave, he shrugged his shoulders and said,

"Okay. So?"

I was not expecting that. He must have been serious because he never brought it up again. He loves me for who I am and does not judge me for who I was.

The surgery made my self-esteem deteriorate. The right side of my facial functions were frozen, and I was so ashamed and embarrassed. This caused me to be angry sometimes because that was the only emotion I was shown my entire life. Any time I yelled in anger and frustration, Rob was there to calm me down. He never raised his voice at me or responded in anger, but rather reacted with patience and gentleness. Soon enough, the anger subsided because of his response.

I would often wonder to myself,

"So this is how love is supposed to be? I wasn't imagining a fantasy in my head, but this does exist?"

Even when I felt unattractive, he always made me feel beautiful. He even made hair appointments with my favorite stylist to help me feel somewhat pretty. This was too good to be true.

Whoever is reading this right now, please understand. If you are anything like me and walked in my shoes, if you are in an abusive relationship in any way,—mental, physical or emotional—get out of that house right now. I am not saying to divorce your husband because this is something you should go to your pastor about and definitely pray to God about, but get to safety. Abuse of any kind is not how relationships are supposed to be. You do not need to be in that hell or anywhere near it.

A pastor of a church I went to explained it like this:

If you are in the Ocean, you are in the shark's territory, and they can and probably will harm you. But if you are on dry land and away from their territory, then you are safe.

If we put ourselves in bad situations and don't get away from it, then we most likely will be hurt. If you run after God instead of that situation, then you will be safe. That isn't to say that God won't protect you if you do put yourself in a shark situation, but it is better for you mentally and physically to be somewhere you can find peace.

Peace. There isn't a better word to explain the peace I am in now. As I type this right now it is early in the morning, because those are the times I have found to be best for writing. The house is quiet, and everyone's asleep, and although that is peaceful, that isn't what I mean. I mean that once there was commotion and turmoil in my soul, and now I am calm. Once there was constant anxiety and fear, and now there is laughter. At one time, yelling, abuse and anger consumed my days, and now my days are filled with kisses from my husband and my kids and love. Remember those demons I described earlier that tormented me day and night and made me feel crazy? Well, they are gone. They are no more.

Love, I finally understand it. That one prayer I prayed...

"God, send me someone who will love me like you."

None of us can love like our Father in Heaven since He is the very definition of love. But Rob was that answer. I will never forget the day God came into my life, saved me, and piece by piece started rebuilding and healing my life and leading me out of the wilderness. Another day I will never forget is when Rob came in and showed me what being saved means. If you have ever thought to yourself that you will stay because you won't find something better, don't believe those lies Satan is whispering in your ears. It's not true. This kind of love does exist. If you need a good model for the love God wants us to have and live by, you can find it in the Bible:

Love is patient, love is kind. It does not envy, it does not boast, it is not proud. It does not dishonor others, it is not self-seeking, it is not easily angered, it keeps no record of wrongs. Love does not delight in evil but rejoices with the truth. It always protects, always trusts, always hopes, always perseveres. Love never fails. (1 Corinthians 13: 4-8)

Today, we live in a beautiful home across from my in-law's house and our farm. Rob and I got married in our backyard before our actual wedding, and the kids were all there. They played in the grass with our German Sheppard, Cinna, where we stood with our Pastor while he married us. It was beautiful. This year Rob plowed and tilled a garden in our spacious back-yard. I've got cucumbers, tomatoes, lettuce, onions, cabbage, broccoli, corn, and green beans growing back there, and they are all doing so well. It's my first time gardening! I love going out there to work on the garden. It's peaceful, and I talk to God a lot.

Rob and I share three girls and a boy and our furbaby, Cinna. I am so thankful that I get to be their Mama. I get to help them on their way to finding their something better. I will teach my children to sing, dance and praise in God's presence all the days of my life. The job I have now is a Godsend and so fulfilling. I am a Sunday School teacher at my church, and I love being able to teach kids the love of Jesus. My husband likes to cook with me, so we make dinner together and share family meals at our dinner table. We play a game called, "Best Part, Worst Part." It's where we take turns going around the table to discuss our best part of the day and our worst part. The kids love that game. Last weekend I was outside working on my garden while the kids and Cinna played in the sprinkler and Rob cooked on his new grill. It was picture-perfect.

I never thought I would have this life. Before I found out it was the Holy Spirit guiding me the whole time, I didn't know why I always told myself to hold on, that there has got to be something better than this. I am so thankful I did. I walked through abandonment, abuse, mental illnesses, suicide attempts and foster care, and trying to fill my voids with men, alcohol and drugs. Then I met Jesus, and He started leading me out. I let the things of this world knock me down and distract me until I fell into a deep pit. It brought me to paths of the love of money, prostitution and a relationship that almost killed me. I came to the end of myself and surrendered, asking God for his help. Once again, God immediately came to my rescue and picked me up and landed me safely on my feet. He helped me heal and gave me the strength to face and overcome anything that the devil leveraged against me.

God restored all I lost: a family, a home, a job and even myself and sanity. I love this life that I have now, and I am thankful for the trials I endured. Being free and on the other side of it now, I am able to appreciate the light so much more knowing what it felt like to be in the darkness for so long.

This is what redeemed means:

"To obtain or release or restoration of, as from captivity, by paying a ransom."[3]

I have been redeemed. Hallelujah! The storm is over, and God got me through my labyrinth maze and into my promised land. Unharmed by the storm and untouched by the furnace, I came out of it not even smelling like smoke. When God allows a storm to happen in your life, you can be sure to see the rainbow shining through the rain clouds in reflection to His light. And when you see it, you will see His promise.

"They saw that the fire had not harmed their bodies, nor was a hair of their heads; their robes were not scorched, and there was no smell of fire on them." (Daniel 3:27)

So I am sure you are probably wondering,

"Well, now what?"

Good question.

---

[3] "Redeemed." *Dictionary.com*, n.d. Web. 2 May. 2018

eight

RISEN

I no longer live, but Christ lives in me.
Galatians 2:20

Though I have fallen, I will rise.
Micah 7:8

*If my people, who are called by my name, will humble
themselves and pray and seek my face and turn from
their wicked ways, then I will hear from heaven, and
I will forgive their sin and heal their land.*
2 Chronicles 7:14

Rise means to get up from sleep; to return from death.[4]

The world did some of its best work on my life. Many times that I fell, I should have never got up. Yet here I am sitting in front of a computer screen typing away, wanting to help someone else, like in elementary school. According to the world, I wasn't supposed to be here. Many people, after hearing a fraction of my story, say

"Why aren't you in jail or hooked on drugs or dead? People with your story never make it."

---

[4] "Rise." . Merriam-Webster, n.d. Web. 2 Jun. 2018

Maybe they are right. The things of the world never give life. According to Revelation, when Jesus comes back, there will be a new Heaven and a new Earth. Maybe that's why God says we aren't of this world, we are in it (John 17:16). I am not of this world and neither are you.

Adam and Eve were the first humans to walk and talk with God in the Garden of Eden in our world. I can't imagine what it must have felt like to know that you and another person were the only humans in existence! The whole earth was untouched by human hands, still freshly designed by God. Not only that, but it was also the first generation, so they didn't have inventions or know different people from different professions. Could you imagine Adam pulling out his cell phone to take a selfie with Eve for his Instagram account, posing and smiling in front of the Niagra Falls or something? Now that I have that picture in my head, I have to admit, it made me chuckle out loud.

Adam and Eve didn't have a cell phone or social media, and maybe they didn't know about sicknesses or worries. They didn't have friends who wanted them to come out to the bar to drink and party all night. They didn't have these things so they didn't know, but you know what they did have? An enemy, prowling around like a lion waiting to pounce on his next victim (1 Peter 5:8). That same enemy used what he had back in those times to distract them from their God: an apple in the Garden. He used the apple that God warned us not to touch because He knew of the harm that it would cause. Satan enticed them and distracted them enough to get them alone, keep them from hearing the Word of God, and have them make the wrong decision, and get them lost in the labyrinth that Satan himself designed. It's time to unveil the core of all evil. Satan doesn't want that, and he doesn't want us to find out his flaw. Satan is afraid. He is afraid of us seeing him for what he is and stripping all power away from him in that realization. He is a liar, and he has already lost. Dr. Tim Hamon, CEO of Christian International, said this:

"It's not about making us look good; it's about making the devil look bad."

That opened my eyes. It's kind of like the video games my husband plays. When he gets a new game, sometimes he is defeated by the other side while he learns its ways and strategies. Once he learns how the other side works, he is able to defeat the enemy with confidence because he already knows what to expect. If we all know more about the enemy we face and his weapons and ways, then we will become more confident in recognizing his works.

Once I got out of the wilderness I was in and into my promised land, I never thought I would be turning around to go back, but here I am. It's like I am standing at the edge of the forest where the meadow meets the tree lines thinking about how many are in there still lost and tormented by Satan day and night. It makes me furious, and I cannot stay here and enjoy my life when there are so many who will never know what it means to live. God led me out of there, and now we are coming back for all the ones still left behind. If I was never lost in those dark and deep places, then I wouldn't have known where to look for others. As I stand at the edge about to start my new journey, this time I wear the full armor of God:

> Finally, be strong in the Lord and in his mighty power. Put on the full armor of God, so that you can take your stand against the devil's schemes. For our struggle is not against flesh and blood, but against the rulers, against the authorities, against the powers of this dark world and against the spiritual forces of evil in the heavenly realms. Therefore put on the full armor of God, so that when the day of evil comes, you may be able to stand your ground, and after you have done everything, to stand. Stand firm then, with the belt of truth buckled around your waist, with the breastplate of righteousness in place, and with your feet fitted with the readiness that comes from the gospel of peace. In addition to all this, take up the shield of faith, with which you can extinguish all the flaming arrows of the evil one. Take the helmet of salvation and the sword of the Spirit, which is the word of God. (Ephesians 6:10-18)

You may be lost out there, but this is what Jesus says in Matthew 18:12-14:

> If a man owns a hundred sheep, and one of them wanders away, will he not leave the ninety-nine on the hills and go to look for the one that wandered off? And if he finds it, truly I tell you, he is happier about that one sheep than about the ninety-nine that did not wander off. In the same way your Father in heaven is not willing that any of these little ones should perish.

Do you know what that means? You are that lost sheep, and Jesus is your Sheppard, and He is out searching for you. So am I. And I won't stop until you are found.

I wanted to be brave and make the Lord proud. I wanted to fight in His army and win wars on His behalf. But the truth is, I am a girl, and the more I wanted this, the more I failed. I couldn't understand why until it clicked. God wants us to be brave and stand firm against the devil, but we need to stop thinking that this is our war and we need to do the battling. We are human. We cannot fight the spiritual world, but we belong to a God who can and will fight on our behalf (and pay attention now because this realization is the whole reason I wrote this book) if we surrender to God and His ways for our lives. If we choose His *something better* for our lives instead of trying to make our own, if we let ourselves die, then the walls surrounding the promised land will come crashing down, and our paths will be made straight. Then we will be victorious in Jesus and rise from the ashes into our *something better*.

"If my people, who are called by my name, will humble themselves and pray and seek my face and turn from their wicked ways, then I will hear from heaven, and I will forgive their sin and heal their land." - 2 Chronicles 7:14

Thank You, Jesus, for making us brave on this journey. Thank you for your guiding hands in writing this book. I may not have been able to write an entire book, but you can do all things. Thank you for all the lives this book is going to save from the wilderness. Thank you for always choosing us even when we don't choose you first. Thank you for leaving the ninety-nine in search of the one lost sheep. Thank you for every tear we ever cried in life, for every wound and every heartbreak because it all leads us right where we are today, and we couldn't imagine anything better than to be right here with you. Thank you for choosing us and loving us unconditionally. Thank you for showing us that we aren't victims or survivors, but we are overcomers.

In Jesus' name,

Amen.

nine

REVELATION

*Write on a scroll what you see and send it to the
seven churches.*
Revelation 1:11

Today I am sitting in a hotel room in Pennsylvania attending
a Christian conference. It's a weekend that both of my girls
will be with their dads, and I heard that a well-known speaker
was on tour not far from where I live. I told Rob about it. He
insisted I go, and it worked out for me to be here.

All of the Speakers are prophetic, and everything they say
seems so Spirit-led. Although they all speak on different matters, the theme they all have is the same. The year 2018 is
bringing breakthrough. God is causing His army to rise, and
we must be bold; this is our moment. The number eight in
the Bible represents a new beginning, meaning a new order
or creation, and man's true 'born again' event when he is res-
urrected from the dead into eternal life. I am not saying the
second coming of Jesus will be this year. But I do believe God
is searching for an army to raise up, and He is preparing us
now for the second coming.

Ever since I was saved, I have had numerous dreams and
visions, some that have come true, some that I knew were

meant to be warnings, and some that haven't happened yet, but I believe one day will. I believe God has called me into the office of the prophet. Some people won't agree with that statement. I wasn't even going to say it, but I sense God is telling me to step out in faith and take a risk. The first time I told someone I had the gift of prophecy, another pastor in the room, after hearing this, laughed at me and said, "What, do you have a word from the Lord for us?" He said that prophets weren't of the New Testament times, and I almost believed him until I realized that God is the same God He has always been yesterday, today and tomorrow. Doesn't it say right in the New Testament, in Ephesians 4:11, that God gave some the gifts of being a prophet?

"So Christ himself gave the apostles, the prophets, the evangelists, the pastors and teachers"

A prophet can be defined as someone who teaches from inspirations from God. Why aren't prophets of these times? Doesn't God speak to His people still today like He used to? Regardless of what I feel God has called me to do, I want to make one point. Everything in this book I believe to be Spirit-led from God to the ones who have ears to hear. I believe He is using me to speak His words to you. He has a message for all of us, not just the ones in the Church.

In 2014 when I was living with my mother before I moved back to Maryland, I was sitting in my room alone and talking out loud to Jesus. I didn't have an agenda or any questions I wanted to be answered. I wanted to spend time with Him. The day He saved me was still very fresh in my life, and I couldn't wait to be in my room alone with the door closed spending time with Him.

I imagined being with Him in the clouds. We were dancing, and there were butterflies because I love butterflies. I always have. It was something about knowing that an ugly, hairy worm, that made girls scream if seen, that once crawled the ground, became this beautiful creature with wings, full of beautiful colors, everyone wanted to be around. That metamorphosis always fascinated me even before I was saved.

As Jesus and I were watching butterflies in the clouds, my

mind flashed to another picture. I was sitting in an airplane, looking out the window watching the clouds roll by, and I knew this was a vision. I looked down at my shirt, and I was wearing a name tag, and I was dressed in a professional outfit. This got my attention, so I asked God,

"Where are we going?"

Suddenly I was sitting at a table signing books for people who were lined up to buy one, smiling and talking to them as they came by. Just as fast as I saw it, it was gone, but I have not and will not ever forget that vision. This was before I ever thought about writing a book, but the Bible says that you will know a true prophet if their dreams and visions come to pass in Deuteronomy 18:22.

Now you know why airplanes hold three significant parts in my life story. Maybe this one didn't happen yet, but it will. I have faith that it will. When it does happen, and this book does what I hope and pray it does for you, I hope that after you read this last sentence and close this book, you will fall to your knees ready to wave the white flag. Our Father in Heaven loves you and cares about you and your life. Surrender to your Father in Heaven. Stop trying to control your life because only He can bring you your *Something Better*.

"For I know the plans I have for you," declares the Lord, "plans to prosper you and not to harm you, plans to give you hope and a future." (Jeremiah 29:11)

LORD, I SURRENDER

*"Yet if you devote your heart to him and stretch
out your hands to him, if you put away the sin
that is in your hand and allow no evil to dwell in
your tent, then, free of fault, you will lift up your
face; you will stand firm and without fear." - Job
11:13-15*

Sometimes, it's not easy to ask Jesus to take the wheel. It can
be scarey and uncomfortable knowing you are trusting a God
you cannot see to take over the wheel of your life and safely
get you on the right path. I get it. I was just there. The thing is
that if I allow God to take full control of every aspect of my life,
He always brings me something better. For twenty eight years
I held onto that steering wheel, and I crashed time and time
again. Until finally, I let go and I surrendered the wheel for God
to take over. In just three years, He has brought me more than
I could have ever imagined bringing myself in my entire life.
Now, I won't have it any other way.

Maybe you have given your heart to God a long time ago, but
you know God is calling you to once again surrender your life to
Him. Maybe you have never asked God to come into your heart
before, and this is something you know you need to do. Either
way, now is the time. Pray with me?

Father,
*I need you. I am so sorry for the way I have lived my life.
Please forgive me. I see now that when I try to take control of my
life, it always leads me to places I never want to be. I want out of
this never-ending maze. I cannot do this anymore. Teach me your
ways. I give you all that I am. Take control; my heart is yours.
Thank you for sending your son, Jesus, to die on the cross and do
for me what I cannot do for myself. I love you, Father. Your will,
not mine.*
In Jesus' name,
Amen

Left: Melissa in 2008 - Right: Melissa in 2015

Melissa's mother, Deborah Roberts, and Melissa in 1994

Melissa on her Wedding Day
Photo by Leah Adkins leahadkinsphoto@gmail.com

Melissa, Rob and their four children and furbaby.
Photo by Leah Adkins leahadkinsphoto@gmail.com

ABOUT THE AUTHOR

Melissa Mattie lives in Maryland with her husband, four children and her fur-baby, a German Shepard named Cinna. Melissa was a lost soul whom God found. Having gone through the furnace in life and coming out unharmed by the fire, her biggest passion is to tell everyone about what God has done for her.

When Melissa isn't checking her many planners to keep up with being a mother, homemaker and wife, you can find her either writing or reading. She is a Sunday School teacher at her church and lights up at any chance to teach anyone of the God who saves. Melissa and her family live on a farm and enjoy gardening, keeping their dog from harassing the poor chickens and, after convincing the kids to abandon their video games, enjoying each second together as a family.

To bring the message of *Something Better* to your next event, contact Melissa.Mattie87@gmail.com.

Connect with Melissa:
Website: MelissaMattie.com
Email: Melissa.Mattie87@gmail.com
Facebook: www.Facebook.com/MelissaMattieWriting

Made in the USA
Middletown, DE
20 June 2022

67471080R00060